Christmas B Boards
Walls, Windows, Doors and More

by

Ellen Javernick

illustrated by
Dan Grossmann

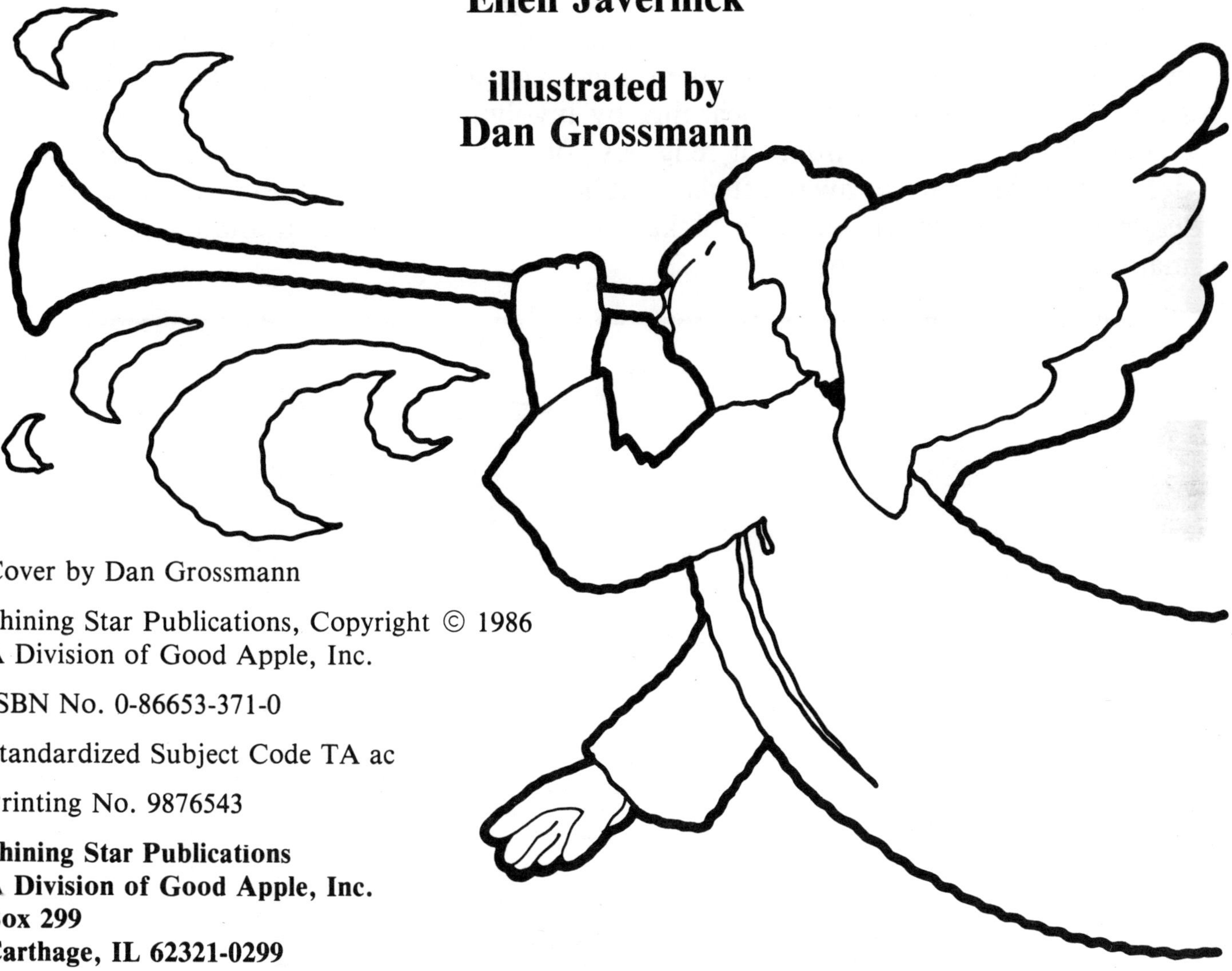

Cover by Dan Grossmann

Shining Star Publications, Copyright © 1986
A Division of Good Apple, Inc.

ISBN No. 0-86653-371-0

Standardized Subject Code TA ac

Printing No. 9876543

Shining Star Publications
A Division of Good Apple, Inc.
Box 299
Carthage, IL 62321-0299

The purchase of this book entitles the buyer to reproduce student activity pages for classroom use only. Any other use requires written permission from Shining Star Publications.

All rights reserved. Printed in the United States of America.

Unless otherwise indicated, the King James version of the Bible was used in preparing the activities in this book.

TO THE TEACHER

CHRISTMAS BULLETIN BOARDS, WALLS, WINDOWS, DOORS AND MORE is filled with ideas for visualizing and displaying biblical lessons in the classroom and is intended to make the meaning of Christmas come alive for your boys and girls. Each bulletin board idea is guaranteed to stimulate discussion, provide useful information, and brighten and animate the environment.

The ideas in this book can employ all the artistic and creative contributions of both the teacher and students. However, it is not necessary that either be accomplished artists. If you find it difficult to reproduce some of the drawings yourself, involve an artistic parent or use an opaque projector to enlarge the drawings. Remember that bold, bright bulletin boards carry their messages best and that when children are making the bulletin boards, the process is as important as the finished product.

This book also contains projects that can be used in a variety of ways. As students complete each project, it can be taken home and used to stimulate family discussions. Teachers who reinforce learning by involving their students in related activities discover that retention of religious concepts is much higher. So, when the decorations are packed away after the holidays, memories of the meaning of the lessons you have taught are also tucked away to be remembered and enjoyed for many Christmases to come!

To my parents, who always encouraged creativity.

Shining Star Publications, Copyright © 1986, A division of Good Apple, Inc.

BULLETIN BOARDS

"And the angel came in unto her, and said, Hail, thou that art highly favoured, the Lord is with thee: blessed art thou among women."
Luke 1:28

From the announcement of the birth of John the Baptist, Christ's cousin and forerunner, to Joseph's warning and flight into Egypt, the Christmas story is filled with hundreds of symbols of God's gift to man, Jesus, the Savior of the world. The bulletin boards presented in this first chapter of *Christmas Bulletin Boards* are guaranteed to help you celebrate the entire Christmas season with more meaning.

An Advent Alphabet	4
Symbols of the Season	5
Stories from the Stable	7
Jesus Our Brother	8
On Earth Peace, Good Will Toward Men	9
Come, Thou Long-Expected Jesus	11
The Land of the First Christmas	12
Joy to the World	13
A Multitude of Heavenly Host	15
A Birthday Gift	17
The Snow	19
By Prophets Foretold	21
Countdown to Christmas	23
Feliz Navidad	27
Priceless Presents	31
Do for the Least of These My Brethren	32
He Shall Feed His Flock	33
Everywhere, Everywhere, Christmas Tonight	35
They Presented unto Him Gifts	39
Prepare Ye the Way of the Lord	41
I Am the Servant of the Lord	43
Symbols of the Season	45
Make a Joyful Noise Unto the Lord	46
I Heard the Bells on Christmas Day	47
Bring a Torch	49
Sing unto the Lord, All the Earth	50
Everlasting Father	51

Shining Star Publications, Copyright © 1986, A division of Good Apple, Inc.

AN ADVENT ALPHABET

A ANGEL	B BELL	C CAMEL	D DONKEY	E EVERGREEN TREE	F FATHER
G GIFTS	H HOLLY	I ISAIAH	J JESUS	K KINGS	L LIGHT OF THE WORLD
M MANGER	N NATIVITY SCENE	O OX	P PEACE	Q QUIET NIGHT	R ROBE
S SHEPHERD	T TRUMPETS	U UNIVERSE	V VIRGIN MARY	W WREATH	XYZ * X-MAS

OBJECTIVE: To encourage boys and girls to focus on the Christian, rather than the secular, aspects of Christmas.

PREPARATION: Collect a supply of old Christmas cards. If you advertise in your church bulletin, you are sure to receive the supplies that members have saved for several years.

Cover the bulletin board with white butcher paper. Cut out the letters for your title and mount them on the top of the board. Measure the remaining space and divide it into 24 equal spaces (6″ x 4″ for a wide board, 3″ x 8″ for a tall, narrow one). Staple down crepe paper streamers for the lines. Use the interior dimensions to cut 24 sheets of paper. On each, write the letter and the word which you want to illustrate. Post these around the room so the children can see them. Explain to the children that you want them to look on the old Christmas cards for pictures to match the cards around the room. When the child finds a match, he can cut out his picture and glue it onto the appropriate card.

ELABORATION: You will probably want to explain why you have chosen Isaiah for the letter *I*. Tell the children that many of the Bible verses that foretell of Christ's birth are from the book of Isaiah. Encourage children to find a picture of a Bible or a scroll.

*Many people believe that the word X-mas takes "the Christ out of Christmas." Explain that the *X* is a symbol for Christ. The *X* sign sometimes appears on Christmas cards. If it is not found, it can be drawn, or a birthday cake can be substituted.

Shining Star Publications, Copyright © 1986, A division of Good Apple, Inc.

SYMBOLS OF THE SEASON

OBJECTIVE: To make the children aware of why we decorate our homes and churches in certain ways each Christmas season.

PREPARATION: Cover the center half of the bulletin board with white butcher paper. Cover the side quarters with red paper. Purchase a piece of holly from a local flower shop. If real holly is unavailable, you can make paper holly. Mount it on one side of the red paper. On the other piece of red paper, mount a swag of evergreen (the bottom branch from an oversized tree works well). Use the directions on the following page to help your students make the small wreaths. Mount them with pins in a circle on the middle section of the bulletin board. Add a large red bow to the bottom. From black paper, cut the letters for the title and fasten them in place. Share with the children the meanings of the symbols you have used. Write the meanings at the bottom of each section.

ELABORATION: The EVERGREEN (pine, fir, etc.) was chosen because it lives when everything else is brown and dead. It is the symbol of everlasting life and God's undying love for us.

The HOLLY, according to legend, represents the crown of thorns. The red berries remind us of the blood of Jesus that was shed for us. We decorate with holly to help us remember that Christmas only has meaning when we think of it in relation to Easter.

Shining Star Publications, Copyright © 1986, A division of Good Apple, Inc.

The CHRISTMAS WREATH is the symbol of God's eternal love. It has no beginning and no end. It never ceases and encircles us always.

ADDITIONAL ACTIVITIES: If any of the following plants are available in your area, you could include them in your bulletin board by dividing the side sections in half.

Mistletoe—the white berries are the symbol of purity.

Poinsettia—Mexican legend tells of how this pretty plant grew from beneath the knees of a small girl. When she had no other gift for the Christ Child, she knelt to pray for Him.

Laurel—the symbol of victory and triumph over death.

You might want to sing or listen to a recording of "Oh Christmas Tree" or the old English carol "The Holly and the Ivy."

SHREDDED WHEAT WREATHS

Materials: two large shredded wheat biscuits per child, the lids from plastic margarine tubs (one for each child), a large bottle of white glue, green food coloring and one bag of red cinnamon candies.

Directions: Begin the project by pouring white glue, green food coloring and a little water into the bottom of a large mixing bowl. This mixture should be the consistency of cake batter. Add the shredded wheat until the mixture is green and gooey. Scoop a glob of the mixture onto each child's margarine tub top.

Have each child use his fingers to make a wreath shape, pulling the shredded wheat mixture away from the center. Have the children wash and dry their hands and then give each child 5 cinnamon candies to decorate his wreath. The candies will stick to the wreaths if they are pushed in gently. Allow the wreaths to dry at least two days. Remove the margarine lids and tie a yarn bow on each one.

The wreaths can be removed from the bulletin board before Christmas and sent home to be used as tree ornaments.

As an alternate activity, the wreaths can be used as Advent wreaths by adding four candles. (They can be sent home wet on the margarine lids to finish drying at home.)

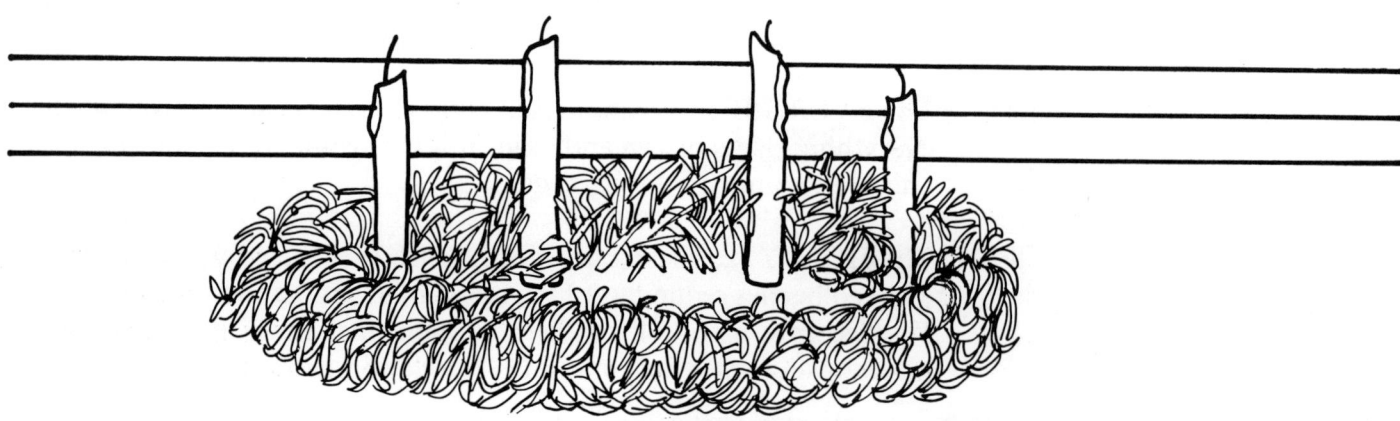

Shining Star Publications, Copyright © 1986, A division of Good Apple, Inc.

STORIES FROM THE STABLE

THE SHEEP	**THE DOVE**
THE ROBIN	**THE GOAT**
THE DONKEY	**THE COW**

OBJECTIVE: To help children realize that we all have different talents and abilities and that we can serve the Lord in different ways.

PREPARATION: Cover the bulletin board with white butcher paper. Copy the pictures of animals from a simple preschool coloring book, or use an overhead projector to enlarge the above picture. With black marker outline the shapes on your drawing. Use colored chalk to color the picture. Use just a little color in each area and then spread the color with a tissue. The resulting picture will be soft and pretty—a pleasant change from many of the bright holiday decorations. At the bottom of the bulletin board, briefly write the legends of the animals you have pictured. Share the stories with your students as they sit in front of the bulletin board.

ADDITIONAL ACTIVITIES: Tell the story of how St. Francis decided to reenact the story of Baby Jesus' birth in a manger. Remind the children that he did this to teach the people that Jesus was not rich but born to a poor family in a humble stable. St. Francis took real animals to a cave and asked the villagers to play the parts of Mary and Joseph and the other characters. Soon other churches copied his idea and made creches using statues to set near the altar.

Shining Star Publications, Copyright © 1986, A division of Good Apple, Inc.

JESUS OUR BROTHER

Read the following poem or listen to a tape of it put to music. (It is entitled "Carol of the Animals.") Then encourage the children to write stories telling about the gifts other animals could give to Jesus. They may want to illustrate their stories.

*Jesus our brother strong and good,
Was humbly born in a stable rude,
And the friendly beasts around him stood,
Jesus our brother, strong and good.*

*"I," said the donkey shaggy and brown,
"I carried His mother up hill and down.
I carried her safely to Bethlehem town;
I," said the donkey shaggy and brown.*

*"I," said the cow, all white and red,
"I gave Him my manger for His bed.
I gave Him my hay to pillow His head;
I," said the cow, all white and red.*

*"I," said the sheep, with the curly horn,
"I gave Him my wool for His blanket warm.
He wore my coat on Christmas morn;
I," said the sheep, with the curly horn.*

*"I," said the dove from the rafters high,
"Cooed Him to sleep, my mate and I.
We cooed Him to sleep my mate and I;
I," said the dove from the rafters high.*

*And every beast, by some good spell,
In the stable dark was glad to tell
Of the gift he gave Immanuel,
The gift he gave Immanuel.*

                    Author Unknown

Shining Star Publications, Copyright © 1986, A division of Good Apple, Inc.

OBJECTIVE:	To encourage boys and girls to use the Advent season to focus on the theme of world peace. To help them think of peace as beginning with them.
PREPARATION:	Cover the bulletin board with bright blue roll paper. Draw the lettering on first with pencil and then with a thick black marker.
	Read Isaiah 9:6. Discuss with the children why the title "Prince of Peace" was chosen for Christ. List and talk about what people need in order to have a peaceful world (food, housing, medical care, educational opportunities, love, friends, freedom, etc.). Ask children to think of ways they can help meet these needs (be nice to brothers and sisters, help friends with school work, fill a Christmas food basket).
	Make copies of the dove on the following page. Have each child cut out one and write a greeting under the folded wing. Give the children silver or gold paper from which to cut olive branches. Mount finished doves on the bulletin board.
ADDITIONAL ACTIVITIES:	Sing together the song "Let There Be Peace on Earth."

LET THERE BE PEACE ON EARTH

Let there be peace on Earth,
And let it begin with me.
Let there be peace on Earth,
The peace that was meant to be.

With God as our Father,
Brothers all are we.
Let me walk with my brother
In perfect harmony.

Let peace begin with me,
Let this be the moment now.
With every step I take,
Let this be my solomn vow.

To take each moment,
and live each moment.
In peace eternally.
Let there be peace on Earth,
And let it begin with me.

COME, THOU LONG-EXPECTED JESUS

OBJECTIVE: To acquaint children with some of the Old Testament characters whose lives and teachings prepare us for the birth of Jesus.

PREPARATION: Cover your bulletin board with a light shade of paper. Use brown or black paper to cut out the tree. Assign your students the Scripture readings found below. After they read their selections, have each student choose a symbol to represent his biblical character. Give the children paper from which to cut the symbols they have chosen. Let the children put their own pictures on the bulletin board. As they do so, let them share what they have learned about the contributions of their characters. The tree your students make will represent a sort of family tree for Jesus. In some churches it is called a Jesse tree because in Isaiah it says that Jesus will come from the roots of Jesse.

Biblical references might include:

Adam and Eve - Genesis 3:1-7	Noah - Genesis 6:17-22; 7:1-10
Abraham - Genesis 17:1-8	Isaac - Genesis 22:1-12
Jacob - Genesis 28:10-13	Moses - Exodus 19:25; 20:1-17
Isaiah - Isaiah 9:6; 60:19	Jesse - Isaiah 11:1-10
David - Psalm 23	Solomon - I Chronicles 29:23-30
Mary - Luke 1:28-33	Joseph - Luke 2:1-4
John the Baptist - Luke 3:11-17	Jesus - Luke 2:10,21

Shining Star Publications, Copyright © 1986, A division of Good Apple, Inc.

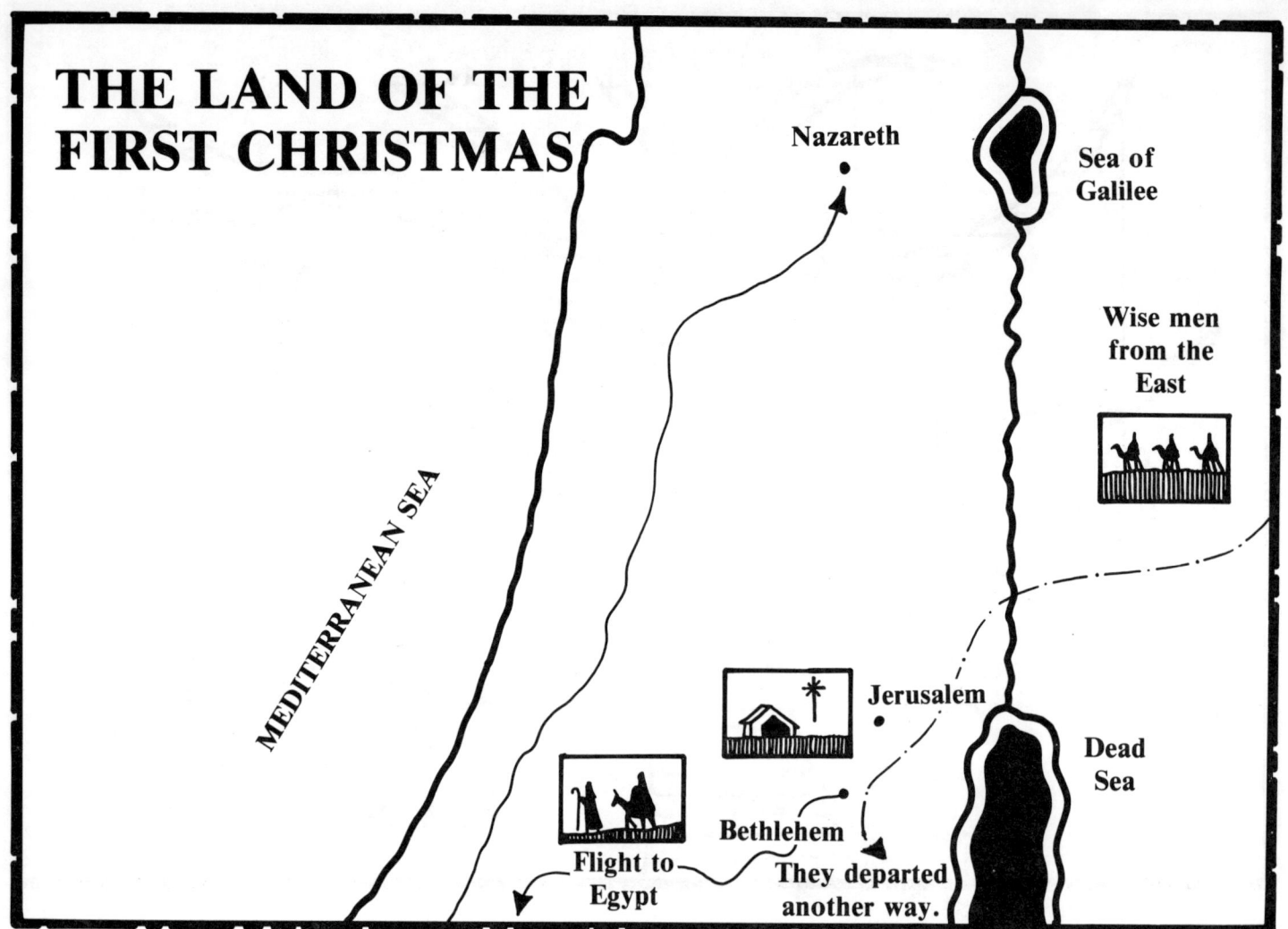

OBJECTIVE: To encourage children to think of Christmas as just the beginning of Christ's mission on Earth and to help them visualize where the events of the New Testament took place.

PREPARATION: Cover the bulletin board with white paper. Use an overhead projector to enlarge the map in the picture above. Use permanent black marker to do the outlining. Make the paths of the wise men and of Jesus and His family. Use colored chalk and rub lightly with a tissue to color the land and water areas. Mount pictures from old Christmas cards and staple them in the appropriate locations on the map.

ADDITIONAL ACTIVITIES: Discuss with the children why the wise men did not go back home the way they had come. Also talk about why, even after Herod's death, Joseph did not bring his family back to Jerusalem. Talk about the prophecies that said: "Out of Egypt have I called my son. . . ." and "He shall be called a Nazarene."

This is a good bulletin board to be put up immediately before Christmas vacation. It can be left up for a longer period of time if your class is going to study the travels of Jesus. The points where He stopped can be marked on the map.

Shining Star Publications, Copyright © 1986, A division of Good Apple, Inc.

OBJECTIVE: To share with children the real joy of the Christmas season.

PREPARATION: Cover the bulletin board with bright green paper. Copy the musical staff on to the paper. Use thick black marker to go over the pencil lines.

ADDITIONAL ACTIVITIES: Read from the book of the prophet Zephaniah 3:14-18, in which he exhorts us to "Shout for joy." Then read Luke 2:10 where the angel says, "Fear not: for, behold, I bring you good tidings of great joy, which shall be to all people." The birth of any baby is a signal for rejoicing so it is no wonder that Heaven sang when Christ was born.

Help your students make angel ornaments to decorate the bulletin board. They can be sent home on the final meeting of class before Christmas. Directions and patterns are found below and on the next page.

BREAD DOUGH ANGELS
Materials: To make 16 angels, you will need one package of bread sticks (found in the dairy case of your grocery store).
Directions: Divide dough so each child has one-half of a bread stick. Have each child break off a piece for the head. Have the child push one paper clip into the head so the top extends slightly (allow for expansion of dough). Have him shape the remaining dough into a triangle and seal head and body together. Put angels on an ungreased cookie sheet and bake in a 300° oven for 30 minutes. Although the angels may be completed as soon as they are cool, you may wish to wait until the following class to decorate them. (continued on the next page)

Shining Star Publications, Copyright © 1986, A division of Good Apple, Inc.

Foil candy paper (like cupcake liners) can be used for wings. Flatten them out and cut. Aluminum foil or the silver paper from inside cereal boxes may also be used. Hair can be made from yellow cotton balls (½ ball per angel) or scraps of yarn or curly ribbon. The cotton balls are easiest for young children. A laundry marker works well for adding features. Older children can use acrylics to paint their angels. Completed angels will last for years if they are sprayed with a clear plastic. (Be sure to use in a well-ventilated room.)

Long sewing pins are best for holding the angels to the bulletin board.

ELABORATION:

There are many references to Joy in the gospels. Have your children locate the following passages in the Bible and share them aloud with the other students:

Matthew 2:10; 13:44; 25:23
Luke 1:14; 6:23; 8:13
John 15:11; 16:22

Kindergarten and primary children would enjoy drawing pictures of all the things in addition to Jesus that make them happy.

Copy the activity to the left on your chalk board.
Ask: Who should be first in your life?
    Who should be next?
    Who should be last?
    What is the result of keeping people in this order?
(Answers: Jesus, others, yourself, JOY)

J__ __ __ __
  O__ __ __ __ __
    Y__ __ __ __ __ __

Sing "Joy to the World" together.

Shining Star Publications, Copyright © 1986, A division of Good Apple, Inc.

"AND SUDDENLY THERE WAS WITH THE ANGEL A MULTITUDE OF THE HEAVENLY HOST PRAISING GOD, AND SAYING, GLORY TO GOD IN THE HIGHEST, AND ON EARTH PEACE, GOOD WILL TOWARD MEN." LUKE 2:13,14

OBJECTIVE: To encourage boys and girls to join the angels of old in praising God and proclaiming the Good News of Jesus' birth.

PREPARATION: Cover the bulletin board with bright green paper. Use black marker to write the verses from Luke. Prepare your students for this project by telling them that stained-glass windows, which originated in about 337 A.D., are often known as the "jewels of the church." Their beauty, like the appearance of angels of old, attracts attention. Explain to the children that they will be decorating the bulletin board using stained-glass windows with an angel motif. When you are greeted with a chorus of, "But I don't know what an angel looks like," explain that no one does. Stimulate their thinking by showing them some angel pictures done by famous artists (check in your local library or share pictures from Christmas cards). After the children design their own concepts of angels, have them simplify their drawings so they can be done stained-glass style. First, have them draw the stylized angel on heavy shiny-surfaced paper and then add "lead lines." When the children have completed their pencil drawings, have them go over them with permanent black marker. While they are doing this, you can be preparing the "stained glass." For this, you will need corn syrup to which food coloring has been added. It works well to have some of the mixing done before class and the "paint" ready on styrofoam meat trays. The children spoon a little of the paint into a color area and then finger paint it to the corners. The end result is a bright, shiny wet look that dries to the touch by the next day. Warning: Do not stack the pictures. When the pictures have had time to dry overnight, mount them on black paper and staple them to the bulletin board. (It is especially effective to cut and mount the children's work on different shapes of paper.)

Shining Star Publications, Copyright © 1986, A division of Good Apple, Inc.

ADDITIONAL ACTIVITIES: Share with the children the meaning that colors have in liturgical art.

Red - blood, sacrifice	Blue - eternity, heaven
Green - hope, growth	Purple - royalty, majesty
Violet - sadness	Gold - holiness
White - purity	Black - the unknown

Visit the church sanctuary. Look at the colors and the symbols used in the stained-glass windows and in the church decorations. In some churches, decorations for Advent are in violet and then in gold and white at Christmas.

Read the story *The Littlest Angel* by Charles Tazewell, Children's Press, 1942. Although this is a picture book, it can be used effectively with audiences of all ages.

Sing "Angels We Have Heard on High" or "Hark the Herald Angels Sing."

Discuss with the children the literal meaning of the word *angel*, which is *messenger*. If God sent a messenger into our world today, what do the children think the angel would say?

Shining Star Publications, Copyright © 1986, A division of Good Apple, Inc.

OBJECTIVE: To remind boys and girls that love is the greatest gift that we can give and to help them remember God's commandment to love one another as He has loved us.

PREPARATION: Cover the bulletin board with white butcher paper. Mount an enlarged copy of Christina Rossetti's poem. Follow the directions below to help your students make one of the heart ornaments to decorate the bulletin board.

ELABORATION: STRAW HEARTS (upper elementary, jr. or sr. high school)

Explain to the children that in the Scandinavian countries people make many of their tree decorations from straw. The straw represents the stable and Christ's lowly birth.

Materials: straw or wheat, which has been soaked overnight, thin red cord, a staple and a glue gun, if one is available.

Directions: (Keep the straw in a damp towel when you are not using it.) Begin by tying three long pieces of straw together. Braid as you would hair. Tie the end with red cord. Make a second braid the same length. Trim the ends and tie the two braids together. (Fastening with staples or hot glue in advance makes the tying easier.) Allow the heart shapes to dry flat. Experiment with this project yourself before doing it with the children. In some parts of the country because of the quality of straw available, you may need to braid a piece of thin wire in with the straw to help it hold its shape. This project takes patience, but once the technique is mastered, children can braid with double and triple strands.

Shining Star Publications, Copyright © 1986, A division of Good Apple, Inc.

DANISH PAPER HEARTS (elementary and older)

In Denmark many ornaments are made of paper. The little heart basket is a favorite with boys and girls because it is frequently filled with treats. The ones on the bulletin board could be filled with "love gifts" (slips of paper telling the services the child will perform).

Materials: sheets of red and white paper. (Old construction paper does not work well because it cracks.)

Directions: Cut two pieces of paper, one red and one white (approximately 2" x 6"). Fold each in half and cut as shown. Cut an equal number of strips up to, but not past, an imaginary line where the rounded part of the paper begins. Weave the two pieces together. Add a paper handle for hanging.

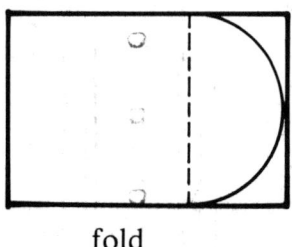
fold

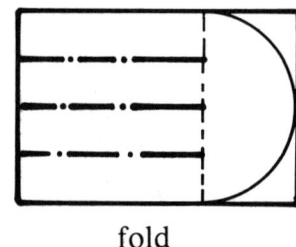
fold

PLAY DOUGH HEARTS (preschool, kindergarten)

Materials: One recipe of dough for approximately every 25 hearts, yarn or hooks for hanging.

Play Dough:

Combine:
   2 cups flour
   1 cup salt

Add:
   2 cups boiling water   2 T. salad oil
   red food coloring

Mix well and allow to cool.

Directions: Have boys and girls roll out the dough so that it is about ½" thick. Use a heart-shaped cookie cutter to make the hearts. Before the dough dries, poke a hole in the top of each heart. Allow the ornaments to dry flat overnight.

*Be sure to remove the ornaments from the bulletin board so they can be sent home with the children.

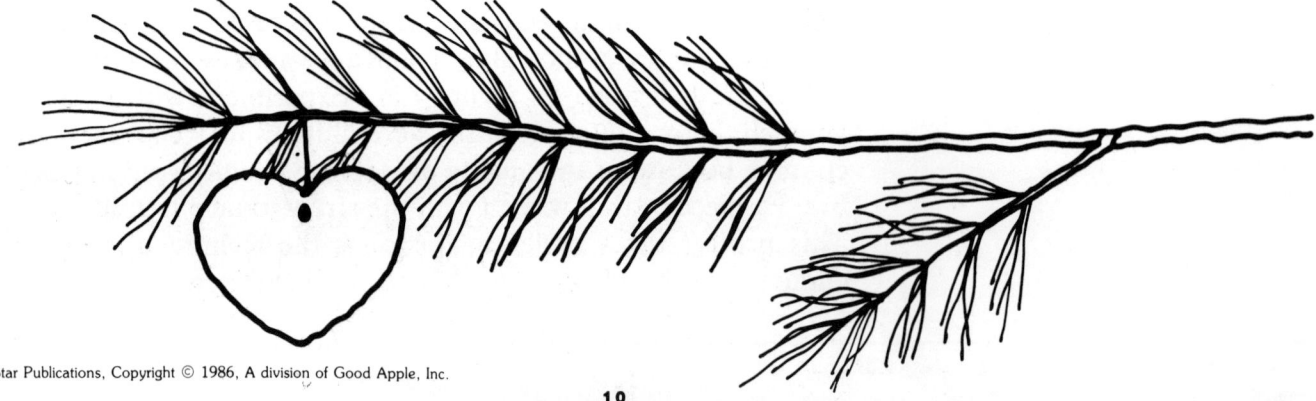

Shining Star Publications, Copyright © 1986, A division of Good Apple, Inc.

THE SNOW

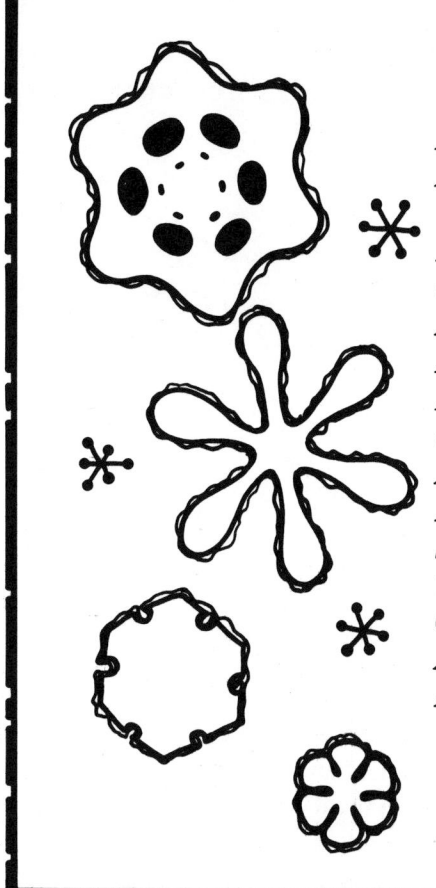

Although we know there was no snow
Around the stable long ago,
The winter snow we see today
Reminds us in a special way
Of the birth of Christ the King
About which men and angels sing.
For the snow is pure and white,
Like the baby born that night.
God sent His Son to free from sin
All people who believed in Him.
Perhaps today God sends the snow,
So modern folks will also know
That His love, just like the snow,
Can cover up the sin below,
And we can all have fresh new starts,
If we let Christ into our hearts.

OBJECTIVE: To help boys and girls see the correlation between God's long-term forgiveness through the birth and resurrection of Christ, and the forgiveness He offers us daily.

PREPARATION: Cover bulletin board with light blue butcher paper. Copy the poem onto white paper and staple it to the center of the board.

Read the poem to the children and talk with them about God's forgiveness. Help them follow the directions for making one of the following snowflakes and then staple the finished snowflakes to the board.

ELABORATION: SNOWFLAKES FOR SMALL FINGERS
These snowflakes are fun for preschoolers because they can do the folding themselves. They'll entertain themselves at home if busy parents just provide the paper. In doing so, they'll pass on the lesson and it will be reinforced by their families.

Start with a piece of paper about 6" x 9" (half a sheet of duplicating paper). Show children how to fold it accordian style in approximately 1" strips. For the first snowflake for each child, use a pencil to mark cutting lines. After the first flake, the children will understand that they should not cut all the way across the paper.

Shining Star Publications, Copyright © 1986, A division of Good Apple, Inc.

SPARKLING SNOWFLAKES

Start with a 4" square of thin white paper. Fold the paper in half carefully; then fold as if you were making a paper airplane. Have children draw designs for the first snowflake and then cut on the lines carefully. Unfold and brush lightly with white glue. Sprinkle with silver glitter.

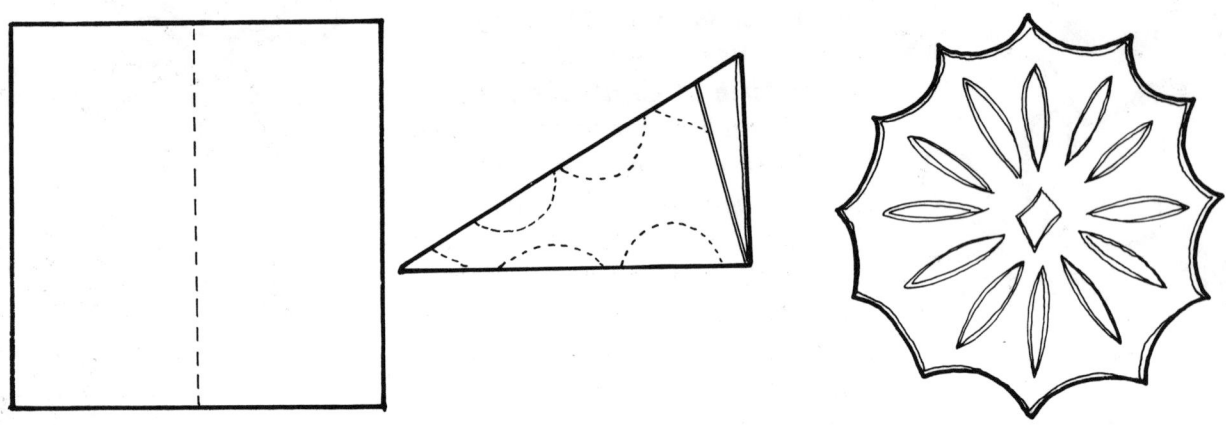

SOPHISTICATED SNOWFLAKES

Start with a piece of thin white legal paper. Pleat it by folding it accordian style. Fold the finished pleated paper in half and cut off the ends. (The longer the points, the greater the expansion quality of the circle.) Make cutouts in the edges of the folds. Open and staple in the middle. Fan out and staple edges together.

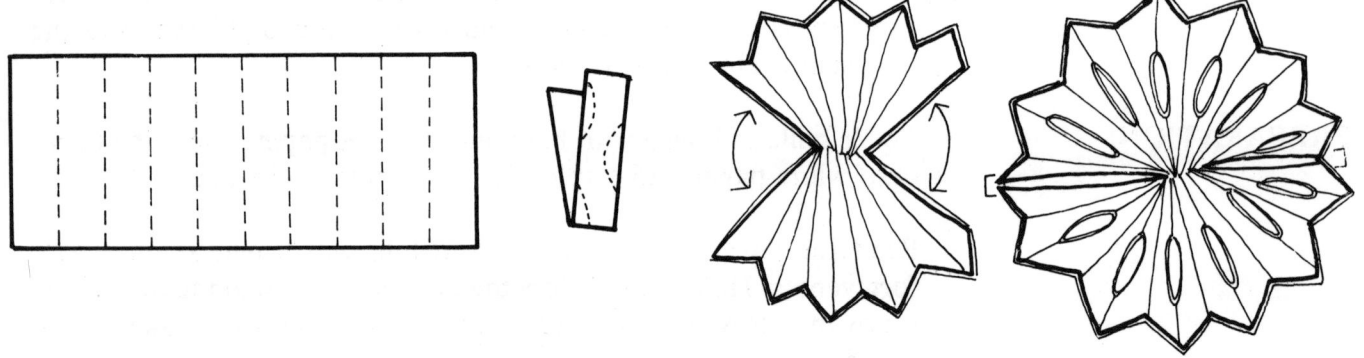

ADDITIONAL ACTIVITIES: Many churches think of Advent as a time to prepare for Christ's birth by reflecting upon and asking forgiveness for sin. Plan a prayer service. Sing the first verse of "Come, Thou Long-Expected Jesus," which asks Jesus to free us from our sins. End with this prayer:

Father, prepare me for the coming of Your Son. Forgive my sins so that I will be as white as the snow. Make me ready to hear His words so that I may see the way to walk, the truth to speak and the life to live for Him.
Amen.

Shining Star Publications, Copyright © 1986, A division of Good Apple, Inc.

BY PROPHETS FORETOLD

OBJECTIVE: To teach the children that Christ's birth came as the fulfillment of the words of the prophets.

PREPARATION: Cover the bulletin board with inexpensive aluminum foil or the shiny paper used to line cereal boxes. Help your students follow the directions for making both the Old Testament star and the Christian five-pointed star. The stars can be cut from origami paper or plain bright Christmas wrapping paper. Use the colored paper for the letters of the title.

Explain that German children often take turns reading Bible verses from stars used to decorate their advent wreaths. Some verses come from the writings of the prophets; others, from the Gospels, tell of prophecies fulfilled. Have your students locate the following verses and copy them onto the six-pointed stars. Have them read through the Gospels to locate where it is written that the prophecies came true. Write the locations of the fulfilled prophecies on the five-pointed stars.

Isaiah 4:6; 5:17; 7:14; 9:6; 16:5; 60:3; 60:19
Ezekiel 34:23
Micah 5:2
Zechariah 6:12
Malachi 3:1 or 4:5

Shining Star Publications, Copyright © 1986, A division of Good Apple, Inc.

AN OLD TESTAMENT STAR

Start with a sheet of paper about 9" x 11" (or any paper of similar proportions). Fold corner a up until it meets edge bc. Cut off the extra strip. Fold the remaining folded triangle in half again. Divide space into thirds. Fold one-third upward (a over b). Fold c under. Cut on the dotted line.

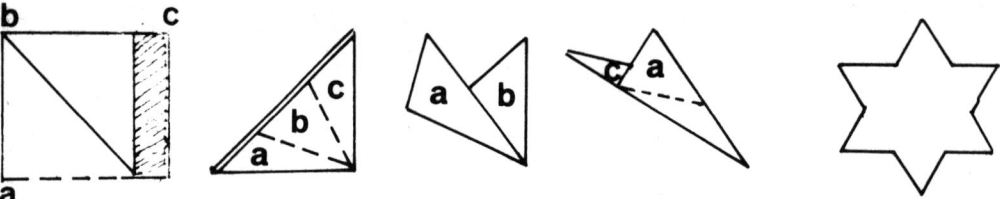

CUTTING A FIVE-POINT STAR

Start with a sheet of paper about 9" x 11" (or any paper of similar proportions). Fold in half. Find the center between points b and c. Bring point a to this center. Fold corner b over along ea. Fold corner d under along eb. Cut on indicated dotted line.

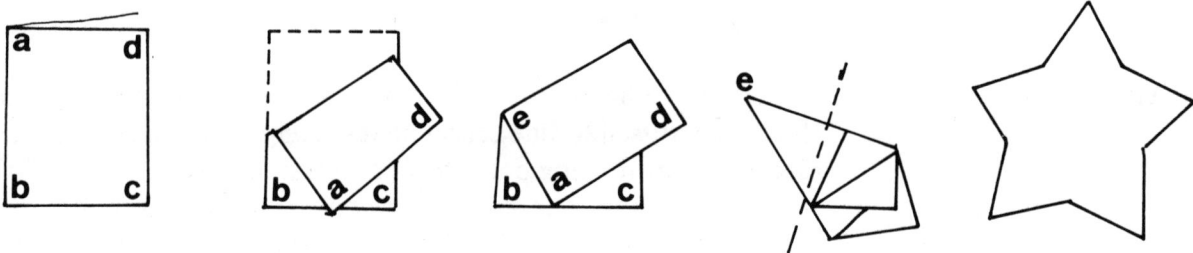

ADDITIONAL ACTIVITIES: Older children would find it interesting to study in more depth the writings of the prophets. This is an appropriate time to teach about the difference between the Old and New Testaments. Children could be asked to memorize the names of the prophets as well as the names of the writers of the Gospels.

PROPHETS
Isaiah, Jeremiah, Lamentations, Ezekiel, Daniel, Hosea, Joel, Amos, Obadiah, Jonah, Micah, Nahum, Habakkuk, Zephaniah, Haggai, Zechariah, Malachi

GOSPELS
Matthew, Mark, Luke, John

Shining Star Publications, Copyright © 1986, A division of Good Apple, Inc.

OBJECTIVE: To encourage boys and girls to think not in terms of how many shopping days until Christmas, but rather of how many days they have to prepare for the coming of Christ. To encourage them to prepare their hearts and minds for His birthday.

PREPARATION: Cover the bulletin board with pale blue paper. Tear a strip of brown roll paper to go across the bottom. Cut a box (approximately 24" square and 3" high) in half diagonally. (If you cannot find a short box, cut the two remaining sides down so they are only about 3" high.) The remaining triangle will be the roof and back wall of the stable. Cover the "roof" with pinecone petals or brown paper "shingles." Use crayons, paint or chalk to make the back wall look like wood siding. From the unused portion of the box, cut a strip of cardboard for the loft. Score it and fold it in half lengthwise. Glue it in place and allow it to dry well before fastening the stable to the bulletin board. In the meantime, make the window sections for each side of your display. Use white chalk to draw and number the windows on pieces of black paper about 18" wide. During the last class period in November, let the children color the figures to go inside your Advent calendar. Mount the window sections on your bulletin board and staple the cutout figures behind them. Center the stable on the board and fasten it with straight pins pushed in right below the roof and again below the loft.

Shining Star Publications, Copyright © 1986, A division of Good Apple, Inc.

ELABORATION: Talk with the children about ways in which they can prepare for the coming of Christ. Let the children make suggestions for things they can do on each of the days of Advent (write a letter to a grandparent, pick up toys without being asked, etc). Before the children leave, give them narrow strips of yellow construction paper. Send notes to the parents asking them to record on the "straw" the ways in which their children have demonstrated their love and concern for others. When the children return to class, they can put their straw in the loft of your bulletin board. (In many eastern European countries, children fill an empty manger with straw—one straw for each good deed they do during Advent.)

If your class meets only once a week, you will have to have the children open seven windows each time you are together. As the children open the windows, help them remove the staples holding the figures behind them. Decide together where each figure should be restapled.

ADDITIONAL ACTIVITIES: Run off enough copies of the figures from the following pages so that each child can have a set. Let the children color the figures. Show them how to use cut-off toilet paper tubes to make their figures stand, or glue the characters to Popsicle sticks so they can use them for dramatizations of the nativity at home.

Shining Star Publications, Copyright © 1986, A division of Good Apple, Inc.

FELIZ NAVIDAD

OBJECTIVE: To familiarize boys and girls with the Christmas customs of Mexico, our nearest neighbor.

PREPARATION: Cover the bulletin board with black paper. Enlarge the Mexican infant and paint it with bright colors. (Traditional Mexican folk art includes lots of clear bright yellow, green and red orange. They even have a color they call Mary's blue.) Cut out the picture and mount it in the center of the black bulletin board. From bright blue paper, cut the letters for the title (Feliz Navidad is Spanish for Merry Christmas). Mount the letters above the picture of the infant. Help your students make one of the following Mexican ornaments to use on the sides of the bulletin board.

YARN DECORATIONS
(For your youngest students.)
Cut light cardboard or poster board into circles, flower shapes or stars, or use one of the simpler patterns on page 30. Have the children attach brightly colored yarn with white glue. (It will be easier for them to work from the inside of the shape toward the outside.) Use a needle and thread to make the hanger. (Older students can use the same technique to create more complicated designs.)

Shining Star Publications, Copyright © 1986, A division of Good Apple, Inc.

MODIFIED MEXICAN TIN ORNAMENTS
(These ornaments are suitable for primary boys and girls, but they can also be made by older students if the time you want to devote to a project is limited.)

Use the patterns on page 30 to make cardboard patterns for the children's use. Have the children trace around the cardboard patterns on heavy duty cooking foil. A dull pencil can be used to press the outline into the foil. Before they cut out the ornaments from the foil, have the children decorate them with paint markers or permanent markers. (It is easier to hold the uncut foil than to color on the small ornaments.) Areas can be outlined in black and then filled in with contrasting colors. Use old scissors to cut out the designs. Glue foil cutouts to colored felt and trim felt to ¼" around the foil.

OJOS DE DIOS
(This project is easy enough for intermediate students but enjoyed as well by jr. high and high school students.)

The Ojos (or Eye of God) is symbolic of God's watchfulness and concern for us. It is used at Christmas to remind us of God's continual love.

For the bulletin board and to use as tree ornaments, God's Eyes can be made with Popsicle sticks. Larger Ojos for use as hall decorations can be made with dowels. Winding materials may be yarn or twine or natural fibers. Begin by gluing the two dowels together in the center. (To guarantee a strong bond, do this prior to class.) Tie the first color of yarn to the center of the cross and then wind the yarn twice around ab and cd. Then wind twice around ad and bc to secure the yarn and form a double X. As shown in the diagram, wind yarn completely around a. Turn frame one quarter-turn clockwise and wind over the top of and around arm b; again turn frame a quarter-turn and wind over and around c; turn frame as before and wind over and around d. Continue until the Ojos is complete. Color can be changed at anytime. Just be sure that new yarn is tied onto the back. To make tassels for the ends of the sticks, wind doubled yarn twice around the ends of each arm. Tie and cut.

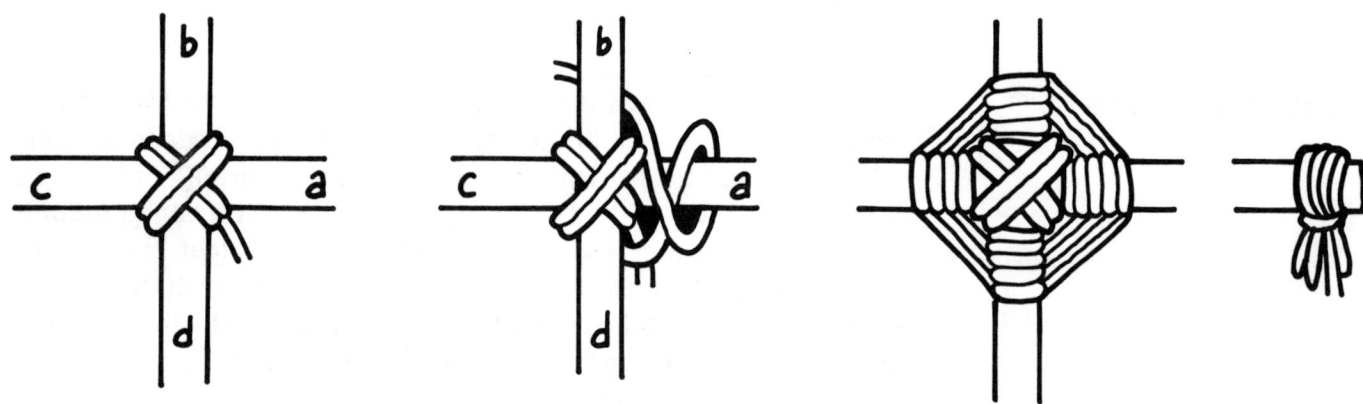

TOOLED METAL ORNAMENTS
(This project is perfect for teenagers. The process is challenging, but the results are very attractive. They can be made and sold by youth groups.)

Ornaments can be made by using the patterns on page 30, or students can create their own designs using church symbols.

Ornaments can be made from 36 or 38-gauge aluminum, available at hardware stores in the form of aluminum flashing. If you are not going to mass produce ornaments, unembossed bottoms of foil baking pans are a free substitute. Work on a stack of newspaper or a sheet of heavy cardboard. Lay a design on top of the metal and go around the major outlines with a pencil, ball point pen or the sharp end of an orange stick. Once the pattern is traced, remove the drawing and reinforce the lines. To make raised areas, turn the foil over and work from the back side. Color the design with permanent markers or paint markers. Cut out the designs with old scissors.

ADDITIONAL ACTIVITIES: Make the piñata and the sand candles described on pages 82 and 85 of this book.

Plan a traditional Mexican Christmas celebration called a posada. Include all the classes in your Christian education program. Children can be divided to represent holy pilgrims and hardhearted innkeepers. A final group can serve as the hosts for the party that ensues when the Holy Family finally finds lodging. Posada means "resting place," and it commemorates Mary and Joseph's journey in search of a place to stay. Although the posada, which begins on December 16th, lasts for nine nights, you can reenact the search in a single class period. Make an image of the Christ Child to be carried at the head of the procession of "holy pilgrims" who wander the streets (your school halls) holding lighted candles and knocking on doors to find a place where they can spend the night. "Hardhearted innkeepers" refuse them lodging. Finally one class (waiting in the gym or social center) agrees to take them in. The procession breaks up and the party begins. The highlight of the party is the breaking of the piñata. The game begins when the first child is blindfolded, whirled around a few times and then handed a "stick" or rolled-up newspaper with which to swing at the piñata suspended overhead. Everyone takes a turn until the piñata is broken and the contents scatter to the ground. The goodies inside are shared by all, and other Mexican-style refreshments can be served.

Shining Star Publications, Copyright © 1986, A division of Good Apple, Inc.

OBJECTIVE:	To help boys and girls remember that the best gifts they can give do not cost money.
PREPARATION:	Cover the bulletin board with Christmas paper (plain or tiny print allows the writing and small packages to stand out). From a contrasting color, cut the large paper-ribbon strips and make a paper bow. Make smaller packages from white paper. Use marker to draw the ribbon strips. Add stick-on bows. Cut the classic letters from black paper.
	Have your students select virtues about which to write essays. Encourage them to think of specific ways of "giving" these gifts.
ADDITIONAL ACTIVITIES:	Change the focus of the bulletin board to emphasize the gifts that God has given us. Read I Corinthians 12. Paul writes that we all have been given special gifts. Read the parable of the talents (Matthew 25:14-30) or the parable of the candle under a bushel (Matthew 5:15, Mark 4:21-25, Luke 8:16-18, or Luke 11:33-36). Have your students describe their talents and write about ways in which they can use them to serve mankind. Sing "This Little Light of Mine."

Shining Star Publications, Copyright © 1986, A division of Good Apple, Inc.

OBJECTIVE:	To encourage boys and girls to share with others at Christmastime and throughout the year.
PREPARATION:	Cover the bulletin board with bright green butcher paper. Cut the letters for the title from black paper or use black marker to write directly on the background. Select several areas of need within your community or choose the needs of your church's missions. Make packages representing the suggestions (a box with a doll to indicate a group that gives refurbished toys to needy children, a vase of flowers to indicate a group that brings monthly flowers to nursing home residents, a shirt box for Salvation Army or a similar agency, mittens for a mitten tree, a food basket, a piggy bank indicating places where there is financial need). Be specific in indicating where gifts should go. Type a list of these places to send home for each parent. Encourage families to select one of these to support.
ADDITIONAL ACTIVITIES:	Decorate an empty box for each classroom to use as a bank to collect money. Use the donations to support a child through the Christian Children's Fund for an entire year. Let a different class write to your child each month when you send the $18.00 check. (To adopt a child, write: CCF, Box 26511, Richmond, VA, 23261.)

Shining Star Publications, Copyright © 1986, A division of Good Apple, Inc.

OBJECTIVE: To remind children that God's love is unconditional and that He, like a shepherd watching his flock, will always lead and take care of us.

PREPARATION: Cover the upper two-thirds of the bulletin board with pale blue paper. Cover the lower half of the board with tan paper that has been torn at the top. Tear two brown pieces for tree trunks and two tan circular pieces for tree tops. Use a sponge dipped in green paint (several shades) to sponge print the grass and tree tops. Make a simple paper sculpture shepherd with a staff. Use a wide-tipped black marker to write the title. Read and discuss the passage from Matthew 18:12-14, which compares God's love to that of the shepherd who loves even the sheep who has gone astray. Help the students make the little lamb ornaments described on the following page.

ADDITIONAL ACTIVITIES: The Advent season is a good time to encourage children to "return to God's fold" by asking God's forgiveness for their sins. Plan a short penitential service. Read these words (from the old version of the Episcopalian book of prayer).
"Almighty and Merciful Father, We have erred, and strayed from thy ways like lost sheep. We have followed too much the devices and desires of our own hearts. We have offended against Thy holy laws. We have left undone those things we ought to have done; And we have done those things we ought not to have done . . . Grant, O most merciful Father, for His sake, that we may here after live a godly and righteous life."

Shining Star Publications, Copyright © 1986, A division of Good Apple, Inc.

Have the children locate the Twenty-third Psalm in their Bibles and read it together.

LITTLE LAMB ORNAMENTS

Prior to class cut toilet paper tubes in half so you have one-half for each lamb you plan to have the children make. Use a needle and thread to make a hanging loop. (Older children can do this themselves.) To save class time, cut strips of black paper with the following dimensions: 1½" x 6" (five for each lamb) and 2" x 2½" (one for each lamb).

Give each child his share of the above mentioned materials and a piece of quilt stuffing large enough to cover the cardboard tube. Have the children begin by rolling four of the strips up tightly to form legs. Cut the top of the legs and fold the cut pieces back ½" so they can be glued to the tube body. While the glue is drying, make a head by rolling and cutting the remaining black strip as shown. Glue two tiny white eyes to the head. Glue the head to the inside of the top of the tube. Cover the body with "wool," pulling to cover it completely. From the remaining piece of paper, cut two ears and a tail, and glue in place.

Shining Star Publications, Copyright © 1986, A division of Good Apple, Inc.

OBJECTIVE: To encourage children to appreciate the Christmas customs of other cultures.

PREPARATION: Early in November send letters to the parents of your students. Encourage them to discuss with their children Christmas traditions unique to their ethnic backgrounds.

On the day you plan to begin the bulletin board, have the children share with the class what they have learned from their parents. Share, in addition, some of the information from the following pages. Allow students time to research the customs of other countries.

Reports for the side section of the bulletin board can be written on white-lined paper, mounted on red construction paper and stapled to the bulletin board, which you have covered with white paper. Cut a tree shape and the letters for the title from green paper. Staple them to the board. If you are working with middle graders or jr. high school classes, give each student a basic person paper doll (see page 38) to "dress" in the traditional costume which represents his/her family background. Clothes can be made by placing the pattern on top of colored paper and cutting around it. Hair can be made in the same way. Have some of your students "dress" the backs of their paper dolls so that they can be positioned in front of the tree. Younger children will enjoy just handing you figures to encircle the tree.

ELABORATION: CHRISTMAS AROUND THE WORLD

ENGLAND (Merry Christmas)
Traditions of the yule log, the Christmas card, Christmas caroling and plum pudding have their beginnings in England. The Christmas tree is set up after children are asleep on Christmas Eve.

FRANCE (Joyeux Noël)
Mangers take the place of trees as the central point of decoration in French homes. After midnight mass, families return for a special meal called le revéillon. It is Pére Noël (Father Christmas) who brings the gifts.

GERMANY (Froehliche Weihnachten)
The Christmas tree and the Advent wreath have their origins in German celebrations. Christmas shopping takes place at doms or fairs. Perhaps they are the forerunners of our church bazaars. The angel on the Christmas tree comes from the tradition in which priests used to give away the Christ Child (a doll that looked like an angel) like modern Santas pass out candy canes. Lubkuchen, fancy gingerbread cookies, are the special treat of the holidays.

GREECE (Kala Christougena)
St. Basil, the patriarch of the Orthodox Church, is given credit for bringing the gifts. He makes his rounds in a boat. Christpsomo is one of the traditional holiday foods. It means "bread of Christ."

HOLLAND (Zalig Kersteest)
St. Nicholas and Black Peter arrive from Spain by boat on December 5th. The good saint rides the skies on a white horse. It is Black Peter who goes down the chimneys. (St. Nicholas can't get his white robes dirty.) He fills the wooden shoes the Dutch children have left by the fireplace. But first he removes the carrots and hay the children have left for the saint's horse.

ITALY (Buon Natale)
Families set up a presepio, a little manger scene, and center their celebration around it. After an eight-day novena of prayers, they welcome Gesu Bambino at church on the Eve of December 24th but receive their gifts on January 6th from Befana (derived from Epiphania), a benevolent witch.

Shining Star Publications, Copyright © 1986, A division of Good Apple, Inc.

RUSSIA (S Rozhestvom Khristovym)
The Christmas Eve supper is a very special meal. It is served on a white linen tablecloth with lumps of hay underneath it. The meal has 13 courses in memory of Christ and His 12 apostles. A large thin wafer is shared with family members and often with the animals as well.

SCANDINAVIA
Families celebrate December 13th as Santa Lucia's Day. Santa Lucia is represented by a young girl who wears a white dress and a leafy crown with candles in it. She comes to each house carrying a tray of cakes. Later in the month, on Christmas Eve, families celebrate with a huge feast, which features lutfisk (dried fish that has been soaked in lye water, skinned, boned and boiled).

MEXICO (Feliz Navidad)
The posada (resting place) begins on December 16th. Each night families search for a place for the Holy Family to stay. On the 24th, they are welcomed and a celebration with a piñata takes place. The poinsettia was first used as a Christmas decoration by the people of Mexico. For more information see pages 6 and 27.

SOUTH AMERICA
Although the traditions differ within the different countries, Christmas is usually celebrated with a picnic. Family members often buy new outfits as we do at Easter. Homes are decorated with flowers, gold and silver figures or clay santitoes. Gifts are given out on Three Kings Day.

ASIA
Christianity is not the principal religion in this part of the world so celebrations are limited. Many of the decorations we use in the United States are made in Japan and China. Decorations made for use in Asian countries show the Holy Family with oriental characteristics and in traditional dress.

AFRICA
The celebration of this festival in African countries represents the influence of the missionaries and combines native ways of celebration with traditions of the countries from which the missionaries came. The Baby Jesus is always Black in religious art of this part of the world.

Shining Star Publications, Copyright © 1986, A division of Good Apple, Inc.

Shining Star Publications, Copyright © 1986, A division of Good Apple, Inc.

". . . THEY PRESENTED UNTO HIM GIFTS . . . ." MATTHEW 2:11

OBJECTIVE: To share with students the story of the wise men.

PREPARATION: Prior to class meeting, cover the bulletin board with black paper. Project the above picture on the board and outline it with chalk. Cut the letters for the title from white paper. Use paint to create a mosaic effect as you fill in the color areas. Dab color on with a stiff brush. Mix a little white with the darker colors of tempera so that they show up better on the black. Use some white to tie the title to the rest of the bulletin board. Make the star in the same way you made the kings.

ELABORATION: Present some background on the wise men. Talk about how hard it must have been to follow the star. The wise men had to travel mostly at night to avoid the heat of the desert and to keep the star in view. It was not easy, and they were probably discouraged sometimes, but the wise men did not give up their search. It is sometimes not easy for us to find Jesus, but like the wise men, we must keep trying. To help the children remember the story of the wise men, have them make small stars for the bulletin board. Give each child a 4" square of black paper. Explain that mosaic is an art form typical of the part of the world from which the kings were thought to have come. Show the children how you used paint to make a mosaic-like picture on the bulletin board. Give them bright paint samples or scraps of construction paper. Have them use these pieces to make mosaic stars. (Paper for the mosaic can be made with holes made by paper punches or just tiny squares.) Staple the completed stars in the sky above the wise men.

Shining Star Publications, Copyright © 1986, A division of Good Apple, Inc.

BACKGROUND INFORMATION

Although no one has absolute proof of their identity, the travelers are identified by historians as Melchoir, ruler of Nubia and Arabia, Caspar of Tarus, and Balthasar of Ethiopia. They were the astrologers and prophets of their day. The gifts they brought and the respect with which they were treated by Herod's court indicate that they were certainly men of authority. Their gifts were both real and symbolic. Melchoir brought gold, a king's gift. His gift has reminded centuries of Christians that Jesus was born to be King forever. The frankincense brought by Caspar symbolizes Christ's deity. It was an aromatic gum or resin used as incense in the temples at the time of His birth. Bitter smelling myrrh was used in medicine. It was perhaps given to prophesy Christ's death.

The arrival of the kings is celebrated on Epiphany (literally appearance) on January 6th. In some countries, the Magi bring gifts to the children as they did to the Infant Jesus. Children leave out hay for the camels. In Italy, Befana, an old woman who legend says was too busy cleaning to go with the kings as they traveled to Bethlehem, is thought to bring the gifts. The legend is that by the time she finishes her work, the kings cannot be found. She is still searching for the Child and on Twelfth Night she comes down the chimney with her broom to leave presents for the children hoping that one will be the Christ Child.

ADDITIONAL ACTIVITIES: Read Phyllis McGinley's "The Ballad of Befana." Discuss her final lines "Good people, the bells begin! Put off your toiling and let love in." She reminds us, as we must remind our students, that we should not forget the purpose of Christmas in the midst of our preparations.

Shining Star Publications, Copyright © 1986, A division of Good Apple, Inc.

"... PREPARE YE THE WAY OF THE LORD ...." LUKE 3:4

OBJECTIVE: To help children see Advent as a time of preparation for the arrival of Christ at Christmas.

PREPARATION: Cover the bulletin board with a light color paper. Sponge print background of grass, trees and sky. Prepare the spoon puppet according to the directions on page 42. Share some background information about John the Baptist, and help the children make the smaller figures for use in the dramatic reading and to take home as a reminder of John's message.

ELABORATION: John the Baptist is the fulfillment of Isaiah's prophecy. He came to announce the imminent coming of Christ. John was a lonely figure. He wore a camel's hair robe with a leather belt. He ate locusts and wild honey—strange food even in his day. He was rugged and stern. He made people feel uncomfortable by revealing their sins and warning them that they had to change. He warned of a firey judgment for those who did not repent.

Shining Star Publications, Copyright © 1986, A division of Good Apple, Inc.

DRAMATIC READING
(Adapted from all four Gospels)

JOHN THE BAPTIST: Prepare the way of the Lord. Make His paths straight. Repent. Change your ways. The Messiah is coming soon.

PEOPLE: (children in unison): What should we do?

JOHN: If you have two coats, give one to him who has none. Share your food likewise. Be kind to others. Do not fight. Be happy with your lives.

PEOPLE: You sound a lot like Elijah. Are you Elijah or one of the prophets reborn?

JOHN: I am neither.

PEOPLE: Are you not then the Messiah Himself?

JOHN: I am only sent by God to prepare the way for the Christ. He that comes after me is far greater than I. I am not even worthy to untie His sandals.

PEOPLE: Why do you baptize then if you are neither Christ nor Elijah?

JOHN: I can only baptize you with water. He who comes will baptize you with the Holy Spirit.

PRAYER: Oh God, help us to be ready for the coming of Your Son. Let us prepare as John suggests by sharing with those in need, by being fair and kind to others.

* * * * *

JOHN THE BAPTIST PUPPET
On the convex side of a large wooden spoon, draw a face for your puppet. Glue on a small bead for the nose. Use yarn to make hair, eyebrows and a beard. Enlarge the robe pattern to fit your spoon. Trace and cut it from a piece of tan felt or double knit. Cut hands from a lighter color and glue them in place. Stitch or use hot glue to fasten front and back together. Use a leather shoe lace for the "girdle" or belt as we would call it today. Slip the spoon into the robe. Glue the neck to the spoon. After using the puppet in the dramatic reading, attach it to the bulletin board with pins.

CHILDREN'S PUPPETS
Run off robe patterns. Give each child a tongue depressor on which to draw a face. Give them scraps of black paper for the hair and beards. Have the children cut and color the robes, then fold them in half, slip the tongue depressor in place and glue together.

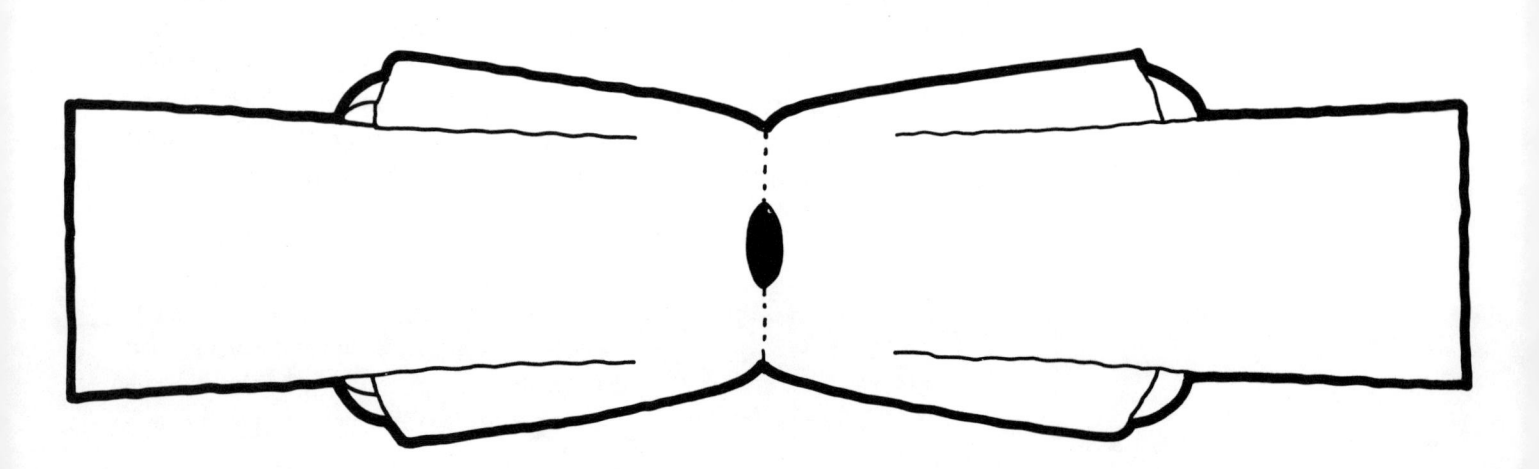

Shining Star Publications, Copyright © 1986, A division of Good Apple, Inc.

I AM THE SERVANT OF THE LORD
LUKE 1:38

OBJECTIVE: To help children see Mary as an example of love and obedience.

PREPARATION: Cover the bulletin board with bright blue paper. Enlarge the triptych pattern, on the following page, to fit your board. Cut gold wrapping paper to size. (Save the scraps for additional activities.) On a piece of white paper, draw or project the three scenes in the triptych. Paint the pictures with acrylic or poster paint. Cut away excess paper and mount on the gold. Cut the letters from black paper and mount them at the top of the board.

Share with the children the story of the Annunciation (Luke 1:26-38). Discuss other times Mary did what God asked of her (traveling to Egypt, letting Jesus go into the wilderness, etc.). Explain to the children that the Madonna was a favorite subject of the artists of early times. They admired her obedience and tried to emulate her love. If possible, show some reproductions of famous pictures of the Mother and Child. (These are often on Christmas cards.) Tell the children that the triptych was often used by artists who wanted to paint three different pictures of a single subject. Tell the boys and girls how early Christians often used real gold on their pictures.

ADDITIONAL ACTIVITIES: Enlarge the triptych pattern on the following page and trace it on oak tag. Have each child draw three pictures of himself illustrating a situation in which he did what the Lord wanted him to do (shared his toys, etc.). Let the children color the pictures with crayons and glue on scraps of gold paper. When the children have finished, have them fold the triptychs on the dotted lines. Show them how to glue a to b and c to d so that their finished pictures will stand.

Shining Star Publications, Copyright © 1986, A division of Good Apple, Inc.

THE ROSE

The rose is the symbol for Mary. Let each child make a rose to mount on the bulletin board. Begin by giving each child four 3″ circles of pink crepe paper and a twist tie or piece of wire. Show the children how to twist the wire around the center of the paper and then pull and stretch the crepe paper to look like petals. Have the students glue the flowers to strips of construction paper and add small leaves.

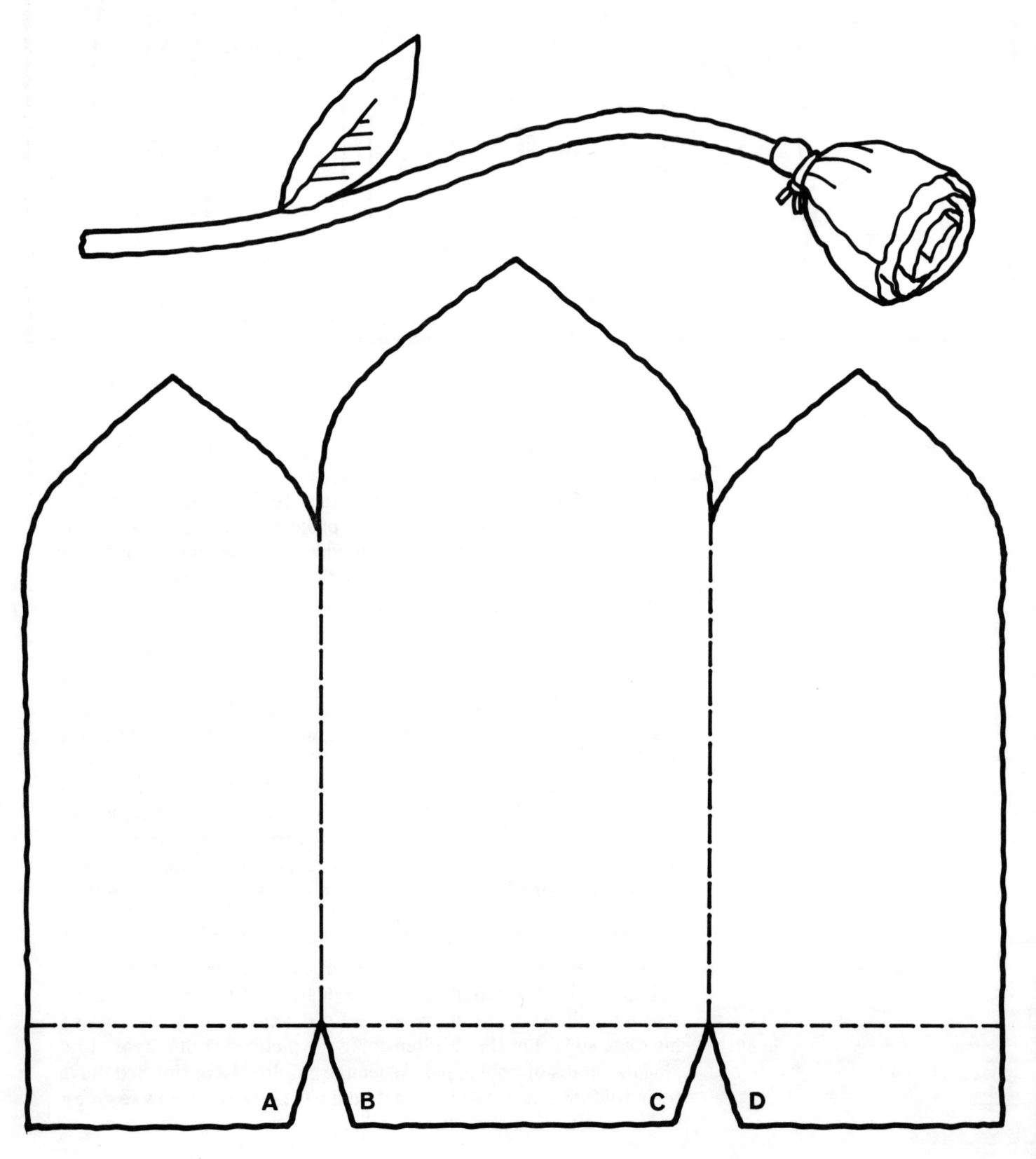

A B   C D

SYMBOLS OF THE SEASON

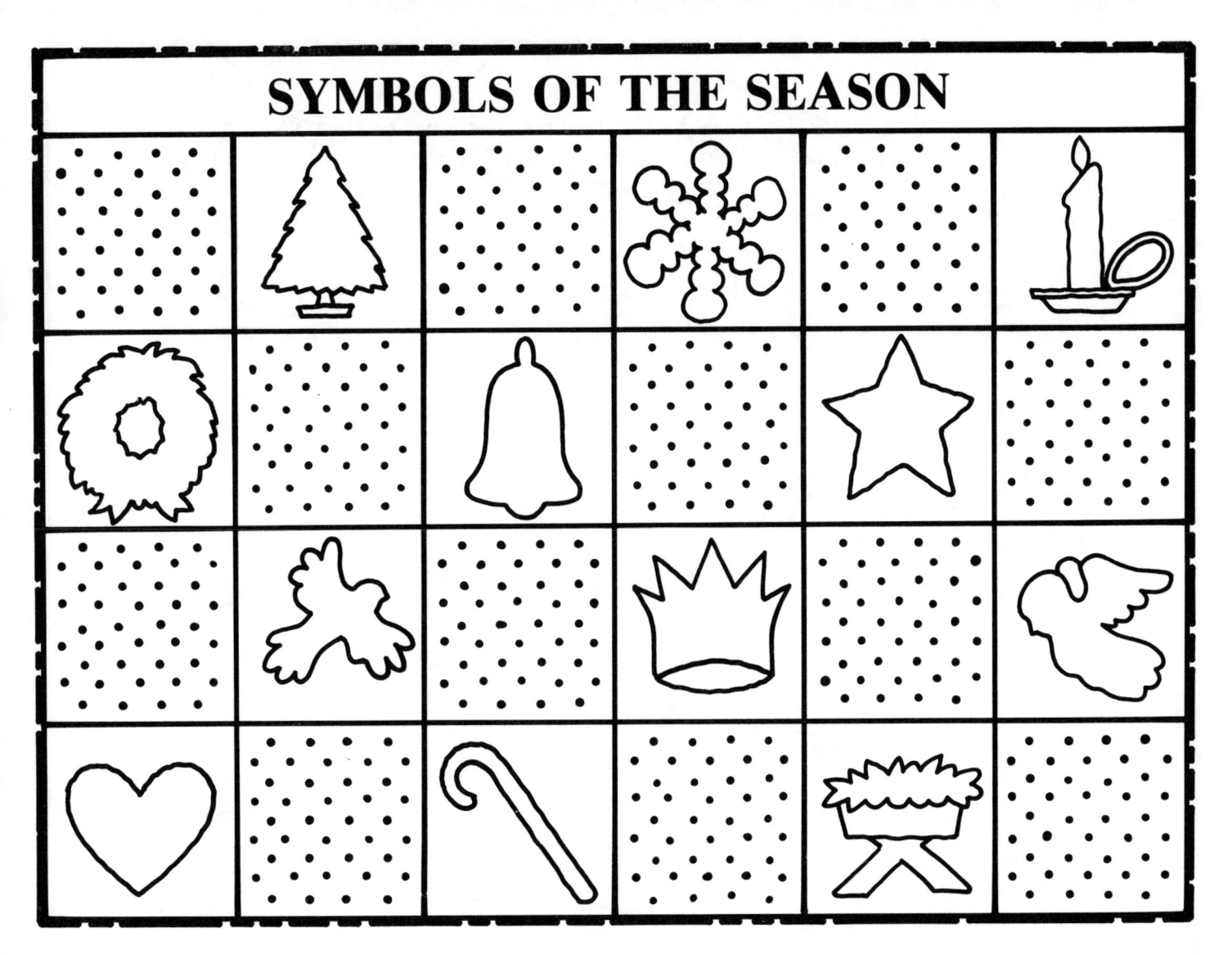

OBJECTIVE:	To familiarize boys and girls with the religious symbols of the season.
PREPARATION:	Cover the bulletin board with tiny print Christmas paper, or use red or green checked or polka-dot paper. Measure the height and width of the board. (Some standard boards are 4' x 6' but yours might not be.) Divide the board into equal sections. If your board is not a standard size, you may choose to make a border around your Christmas quilt because it is important that all the squares are the same size. Since alternating squares will have patterns in them, you will need to cut half of the total number of squares from white paper. Have the children design their owns symbols or use some of the patterns that are included in this book. After the symbols have been selected, have the children cut them from solid red or green paper (pick only one color). Glue them into place in the correct areas of the bulletin board.
ADDITIONAL ACTIVITIES:	Run off a copy of the bulletin board pattern above. Let each child take one home as a greeting card. Fold the paper in half and write a Christmas message inside.

Shining Star Publications, Copyright © 1986, A division of Good Apple, Inc.

"MAKE A JOYFUL NOISE UNTO THE LORD...." PSALM 100:1

OBJECTIVE: To encourage students to join in praising the Lord through the music of the season.

PREPARATION: Cover the bulletin board with bright green paper. Cut letters from white paper. Brush on glue and sprinkle with gold glitter. Enlarge the instrument patterns on oak tag. Let the children use them to trace the shapes onto gold wrapping paper. After instruments have been cut, gold embroidery floss can be glued on to make the strings. (If you want to use the instruments as tree ornaments, have the children glue gold paper to both sides of lightweight cardboard and cut instruments from that.)

ADDITIONAL ACTIVITIES: Talk with your students about how music is used to praise the Lord. Read Psalm 150 together. Sing "It Came upon a Midnight Clear."

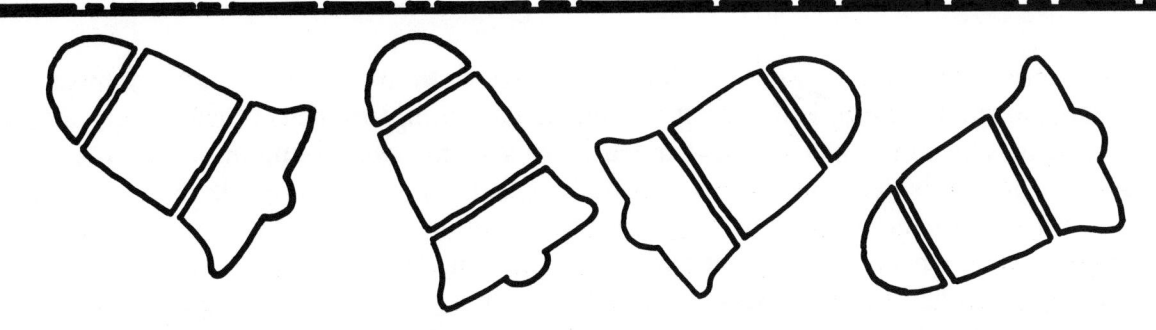

I HEARD THE BELLS ON CHRISTMAS DAY

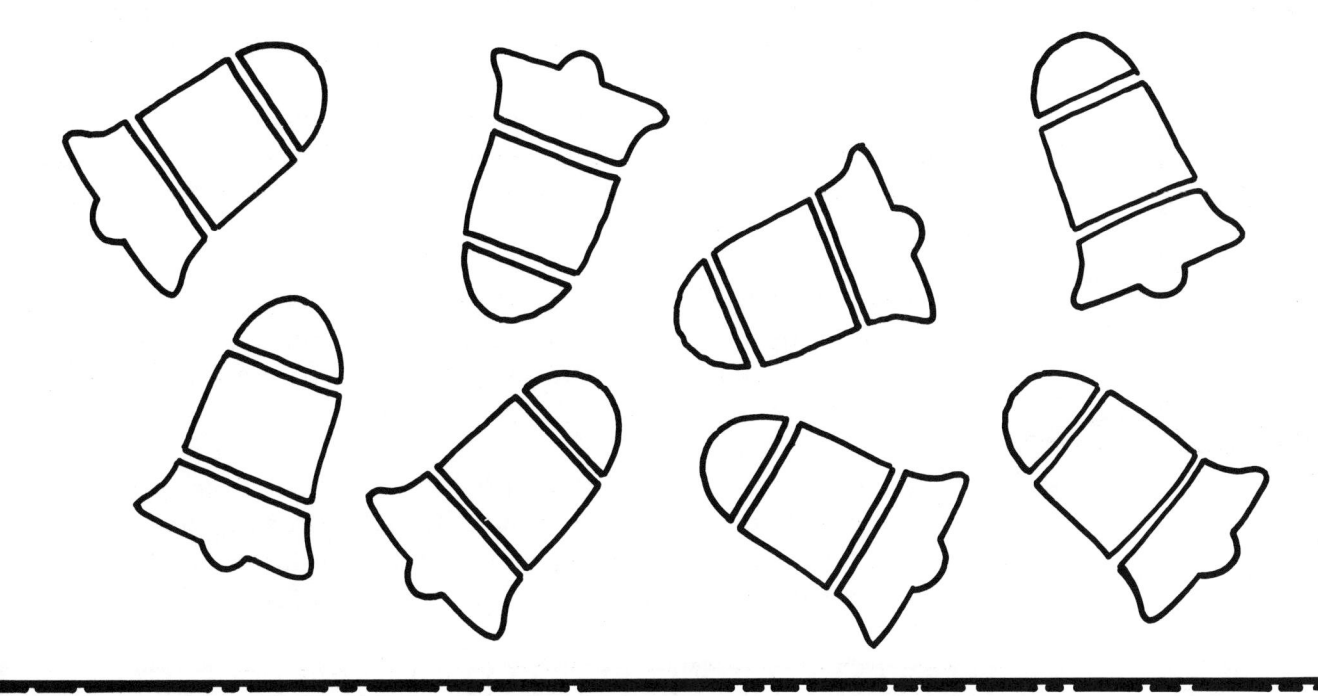

OBJECTIVE: To encourage children to think of the true meaning of Christmas each time they hear the sound of Christmas bells.

PREPARATION: Share some of the background information about bells with your boys and girls. Then measure white roll paper to fit your bulletin board. Lay the paper on a large table or on the floor. Cut a potato in half and then cut away potato to make a bell-shaped stamp. (For a more detailed bell, use a linoleum block.) Blot off potato juice. Paint the cut surface with red paint. Let your students use the potato stamp to cover the background with bells. (With younger children, allow a few practices before you have them stamp on the good paper. When the bell prints are dry, mount the paper on the board. Cut the letters from block paper and fasten them in place on the board.

ELABORATION: Long before Christ was born, bells were used to announce important events, so it is no wonder that Christians wanted to use bells to tell the world about Christ. Until Constantine became the Emperor of Rome, they dared not ring even the smallest bells to announce their worship services. If they were discovered, Christians were killed.

When people were at last free to worship Christ, they were summoned to church by boys who ran through the streets ringing hand bells. Soon bishops began mounting bells outside their churches to announce services. The sound of the bells carried further if they were hung up high. As bell makers made larger and larger bells, churches had to build bell towers. Soon one bell did not seem like enough, and bells of different sizes making different sounds were mounted in the towers. These groups of bells, called carillons, were not rung, but were played instead by hand on a piano-styled keyboard. People enjoyed the bell music so much that many churches started bell choirs. White-gloved members of the choirs rang their hand bells for concerts.

ADDITIONAL ACTIVITIES: Invite a bell choir to play for your class or find out who plays the outside bells at your church and have them give you a concert.

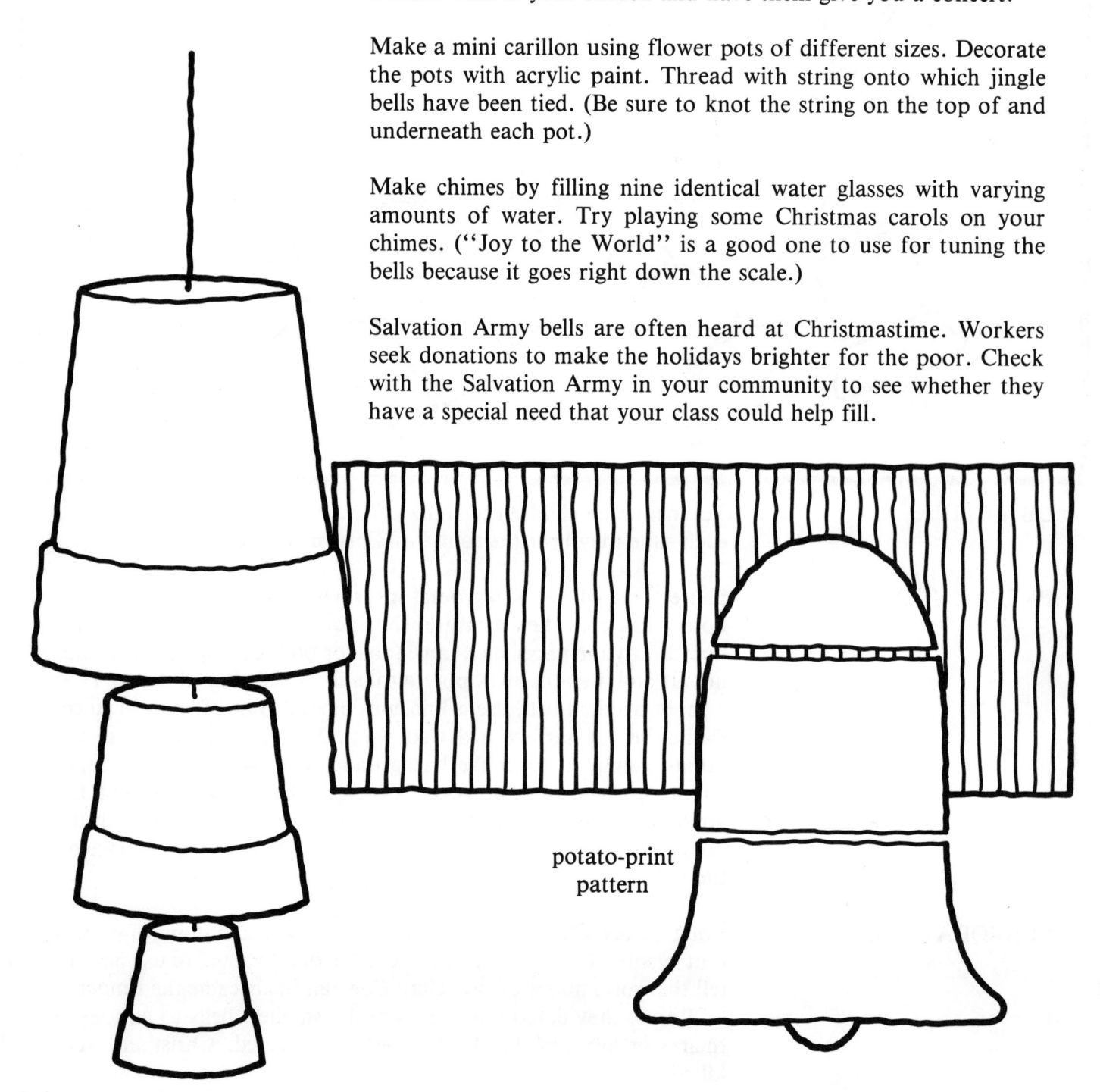

Make a mini carillon using flower pots of different sizes. Decorate the pots with acrylic paint. Thread with string onto which jingle bells have been tied. (Be sure to knot the string on the top of and underneath each pot.)

Make chimes by filling nine identical water glasses with varying amounts of water. Try playing some Christmas carols on your chimes. ("Joy to the World" is a good one to use for tuning the bells because it goes right down the scale.)

Salvation Army bells are often heard at Christmastime. Workers seek donations to make the holidays brighter for the poor. Check with the Salvation Army in your community to see whether they have a special need that your class could help fill.

potato-print pattern

BRING A TORCH

OBJECTIVE: To make the birth of Baby Jesus real for your smallest students.

PREPARATION: Cover the bulletin board with black paper. Cut out white letters for the title. Before proceeding, take your preschoolers to see the manger scene that has been set up in the sanctuary or outside the church. Retell the story of Christ's birth. Encourage the children to share what they have seen by retelling the story to their parents when they come to pick them up. Sing or listen to a recording of "Bring a Torch, Jeanette Isabella." Have each child draw a picture showing how they looked as they "hurried to the stable." Mount the self-portraits below the title on the dark bulletin board.

ADDITIONAL ACTIVITIES: To reinforce this lesson, have the children make candles from cardboard tubes. Yellow cotton balls can serve as safe flames. As an alternative, children can make lanterns by folding a 9" x 12" sheet of construction paper in half lengthwise and making a series of cuts from the folded side to within one inch of the open edge. The final strip can be cut off to serve as a handle.

Bring a torch Jeanette Isabella
Bring a torch; come hurry and run.
To the stable good folk of the village,
Christ is born and Mary's calling.
Ah, ah, beautiful is the mother,
Ah, ah, beautiful is the son.
     (Traditional 17th century carol)

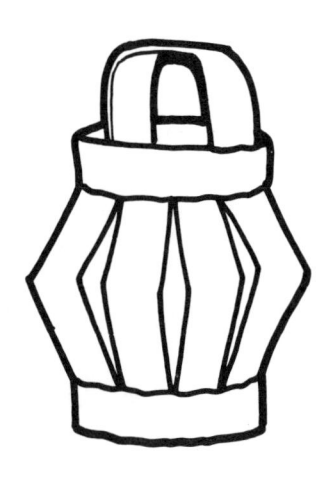

Shining Star Publications, Copyright © 1986, A division of Good Apple, Inc.

SING UNTO THE LORD, ALL THE EARTH.   PSALM 96:1

OBJECTIVES: To let even the youngest members of the congregation feel that they are part of the Christmas celebration and to teach them that singing is one of the ways in which we praise the Lord.

PREPARATION: Cover the bulletin board with dark blue or black paper. Cut the letters for the Bible verse and mount them to the board. Make the simple stained-glass window in the following way. Cut the entire window shape from light blue paper; cut the large circle from red, the small circle from yellow, the bottom rectangle from green and the top triangle from purple. Staple or glue the pieces in place. Use a black marker to draw on the "lead." Make the window frame from brown or grey paper.

Have the children draw self-portraits (heads only). Staple them to the board. Add white paper robes and red paper bows.

ADDITIONAL ACTIVITIES: Let your class participate in the musical mural program on pages 58-62 of this book. Have a class sing-a-long or plan a field trip to sing at a nursing home.

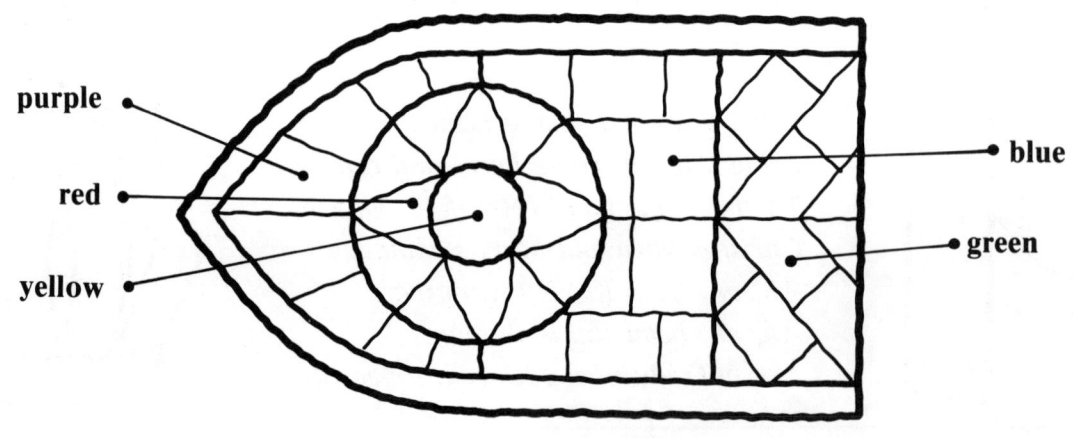

- purple
- red
- yellow
- blue
- green

Shining Star Publications, Copyright © 1986, A division of Good Apple, Inc.

WONDERFUL   **COUNSELLOR**

MIGHTY GOD
EVERLASTING FATHER
IHS
PRINCE OF PEACE

OBJECTIVE: To add to the children's understanding of the Lord and His relationship to them.

PREPARATION: Cover the bulletin board with dark green paper. Cut out large white block letters for the words.

Share with your students the origin of the Chrismons, and help each child make one for the bulletin board. To make the Chrismons, you will need white oak tag and gold glitter. You can make the Chrismons even fancier with the addition of sequins, tiny beads and miniature dried flowers. Be sure to stick to gold and white. White suggests our Lord's purity and perfection, and gold represents His power and majesty. With younger children you will need to cut out some simple shapes for them to decorate with glitter. Older children can do their own cutting and create unique decorations using the materials you provide. When the children finish their Chrismons, they can fasten them to the bulletin board. (The Chrismons can be made from styrofoam meat trays if you want the children to take them home as Christmas tree ornaments. Be sure to have them decorate both sides.)

ELABORATION: Chrismons were first made in 1957 by Francis Spencer. Mrs. Spencer was in charge of decorating her church and she wanted to choose ornaments that would honor the Lord. She came across designs used by early Christians on doors, buildings and catacombs.

Shining Star Publications, Copyright © 1986, A division of Good Apple, Inc.

At that time Christians were outlawed from worshipping, and the signs were almost a secret code used by the faithful to identify themselves and announce their meetings. Mrs. Spencer used these old designs for her ornaments. Over the years other people have designed their own Chrismons or "Christ monograms."

The Latin cross is most commonly used to represent the Lord's saving work.

The descending dove reminds us of the Holy Spirit.

The triquetra represents the Trinity (God in three persons).

The Greek word for fish, *Ichthus*, stands for the first letters of Jesus Christ, God's Son and Savior.

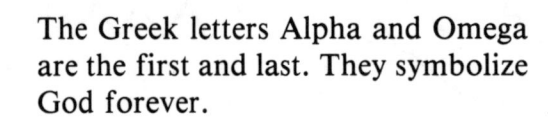

The Greek letters Alpha and Omega are the first and last. They symbolize God forever.

IHS are the first three letters of Jesus in Greek.

The butterfly is a symbol of the Lord's resurrection.

The *XP* are the first two letters of Christ in Greek.

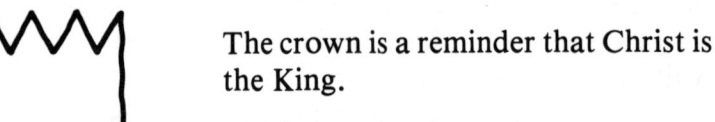

The crown is a reminder that Christ is the King.

The shepherd's crook reminds us that the Lord is our shepherd.

The bread is the symbol of Jesus. Jesus was called the bread of life.

The chalice is a symbol of God with us.

The cross and orb remind us of Christ in the world.

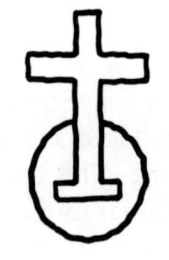

The Creator's star represents God's star with six points representing creation.

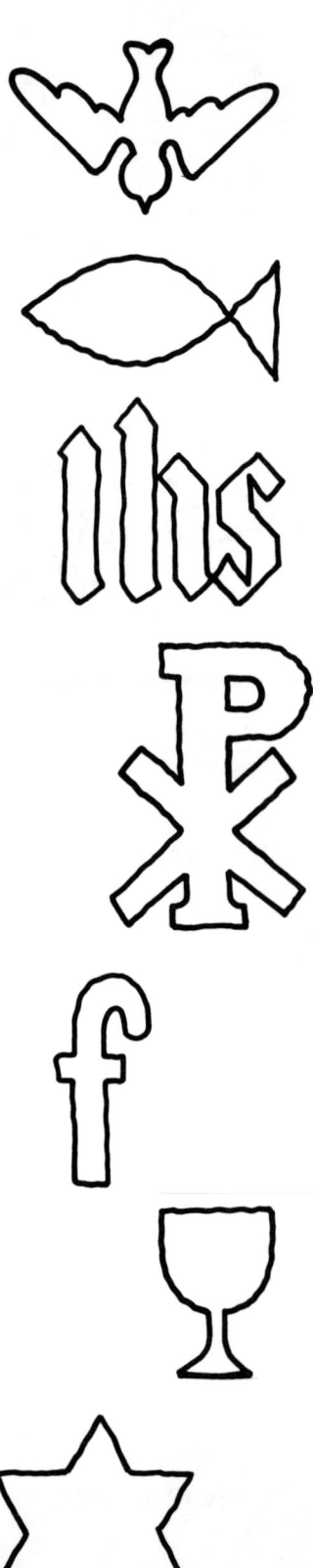

HALLS AND WALLS

"... ye shall celebrate...." Lev. 23:41

"And he set the cherubims within the inner house: and they stretched forth the wings of the cherubims, so that the wing of the one touched the one wall, and the wing of the other cherub touched the other wall; and their wings touched one another in the midst of the house." (I Kings 6:27) This Christmas, decorate your classroom with angels, stockings, gingerbodies or any one of murals or banners found on the following pages.

The Stockings Were Hung 54,55

Banner Basics 56

Junior High Hang-outs 57

A Progressive Prayer Service 58-62

Bright Ideas for Big Spaces 63

Giant Gingerbodies 64

Shining Star Publications, Copyright © 1986, A division of Good Apple, Inc.

THE STOCKINGS WERE HUNG

According to legend the first stockings were filled accidently when St. Nicholas tossed money down the chimney and it landed in stockings hanging to dry by the fire.

You can use these stockings to store Bible verse memory cards. First, give every child a needle threaded with white yarn and two prepunched stockings cut from red construction paper. Have children lace their stockings. They can use white chalk to label and decorate their stockings. Hang the stockings in the hall outside your classroom. Hand out the Bible verse stars (found on page 55). As the children memorize the verses, let them stick the stars into their stockings. At your last meeting before Christmas vacation, place small gifts or candy canes in the stockings of the children.

If you are working with younger children, you will probably want to write out simpler verses so the children will not have to look them up in the Bible. Preschoolers could probably only handle one verse each of the four weeks of Advent.

Shining Star Publications, Copyright © 1986, A division of Good Apple, Inc.

BIBLE MEMORY VERSES

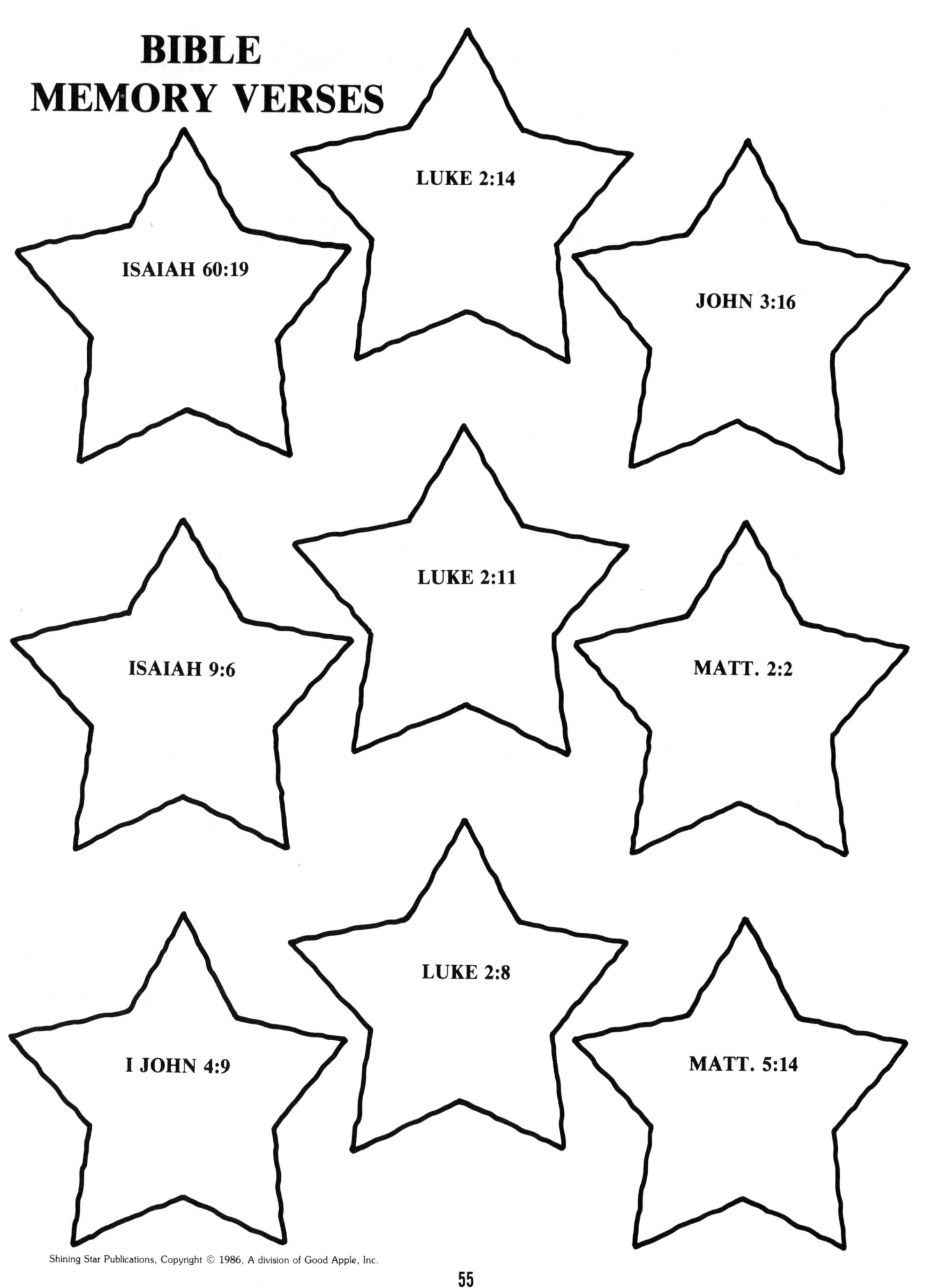

- LUKE 2:14
- ISAIAH 60:19
- JOHN 3:16
- LUKE 2:11
- ISAIAH 9:6
- MATT. 2:2
- LUKE 2:8
- I JOHN 4:9
- MATT. 5:14

BANNER BASICS

When making a banner with boys and girls, keep these basic rules in mind.

1. Make it BRIEF—just a single word or picture will convey the message.

2. Make it BIG and BRIGHT and BOLD—it should be easily read from a distance.

Paper banners are easiest to hang in halls because they are lightweight. Try some of these ideas with your students.

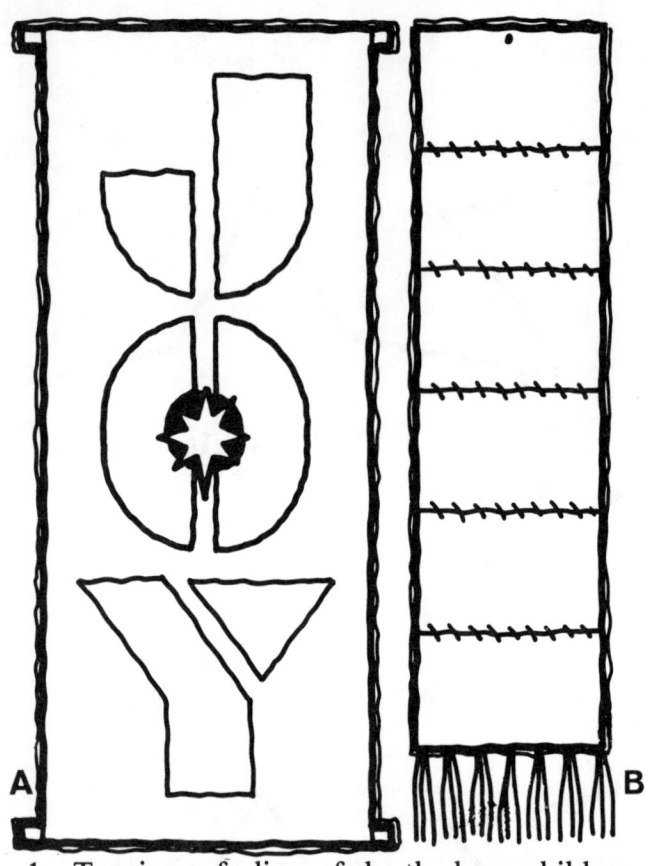

1. To give a feeling of depth, have children cut two large pieces of paper, the same size but of different colors. Cut the letters out of the top piece. Fill o's with pictures cut from Christmas cards (A)

2. Let children sew Christmas cards together and add yarn fringe. Be sure card widths all match. (B)

3. Encourage your boys and girls to choose Bible verses to illustrate in preschool colorbook style. (C)

4. Glue tissue paper to a white background. Overlap colors. Use a black marker to write the words. (D)

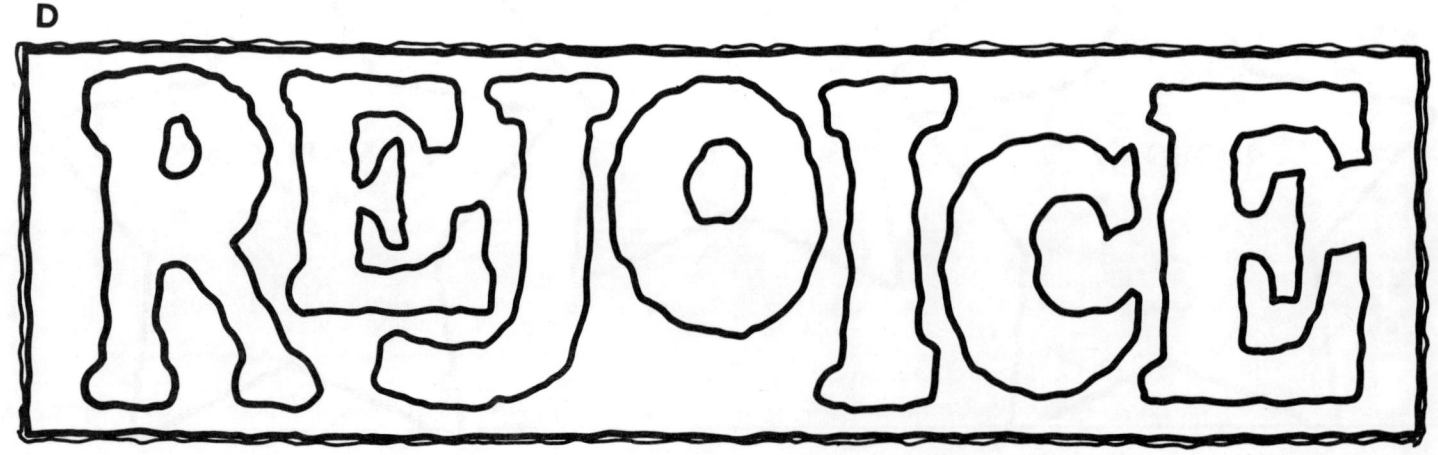

Shining Star Publications, Copyright © 1986, A division of Good Apple, Inc.

JUNIOR HIGH HANG-OUTS

BATIK BANNERS

Have your students design banners bearing messages of the season. Old Christmas cards often offer good ideas. Emphasize how important lettering is in the construction of an effective banner. Give each student a piece of an ironed sheet approximately 12" x 24". (Banners can be larger if you have sufficient space to display them and adequate time to make them.) Have students sew under a 1" strip at both top and bottom. Trace the designs and go over the lines with black laundry marker. Place a single banner on an electric food-warming tray or on an electric griddle with the heat at the lowest setting). Use crayons to color the designs on the banners. The colors will melt into the cloth. Dip complete banners into diluted food coloring. Iron again. Slip a slat from an old window shade through the top of the banner and tie a string to both ends of the slat for hanging on the wall.

POSTERS WITH A PURPOSE

Talk with your students about the posters they use to announce coming events at their schools. Let them list information that posters can be used to convey. Have your students make posters to announce Christ's coming. Be sure to have them include Christ's qualifications and tell what He will do when He arrives. Bright wide-tip markers make it easy for students to complete their posters in a single class period.

A PROGRESSIVE PRAYER SERVICE

On the following pages, you will find murals to decorate the walls of your christian education center. With each picture is a short prayer service. Individual classes can progress from one prayer station to the next, or you can use the murals as a backdrop for a program involving all your students. Each class can present a segment. Since each mural has a corresponding hymn, you will probably want to run off enough copies of the words so that everyone can join in the singing. To make the murals, enlarge the patterns onto five pieces of bright-colored paper. Carefully cut out the area under the star on each page. Mount the colored paper on white paper, allowing a four-inch border. Use a wide black marker to go over the lines. Mount the murals high on the wall so they will not be blocked by children standing in front of them. Be sure to leave sufficient space between murals so that the children can group around each one as they move through the hall.

LEADER: Read Luke 2:1-5
Sing together "O Little Town of Bethlehem."

LEADER: The song that we just sang is one of the most popular of all American Christmas carols. It was written by a young minister after he spent a night in the starlit hills of Palestine overlooking Bethlehem. He wrote the poem for his Sunday school children. The organist of his church had a dream about angels singing the poem. He woke up and wrote down the melody he heard in his dream. It fit so perfectly with the words the minister had written that he was convinced the carol was a gift from heaven.

PRAYER: Dear God, help us during this exciting season to take time to be still and to think of the real meaning of Christmas. Prepare us to let the "dear Christ" enter into our hearts and our lives.

Shining Star Publications, Copyright © 1986, A division of Good Apple, Inc.

PRAYER: Dear God, help us during this exciting season to take time to be still and to think of the real meaning of Christmas. Prepare us to let the "dear Christ" enter into our hearts and our lives.

LEADER: Read Luke 2: 6, 7.

Sing together "Away in the Manger."

LEADER: "Away in the Manger" is often called the cradle hymn. It was sung to little children not only at Christmastime, but as a lullaby throughout the whole year. It must have been hard for Jesus to sleep in the scratchy straw in the stable. Even though the noises of the animals woke Him, He did not cry or complain.

PRAYER: Dear Lord, help us to be like Baby Jesus and not complain when things aren't going exactly the way we want them to.

Shining Star Publications, Copyright © 1986, A division of Good Apple, Inc.

LEADER: Read Luke 2:8.

Sing together "While Shepherds Watched Their Flocks."

LEADER: "While Shepherds Watched Their Flocks" is a very old Christmas carol. It was written before 1700 by Nahum Tate, who was the poet laureate for King William III of England. The words of this carol remind us of the long ago night when shepherds heard the first Christmas carol. God does not often send angels to carry His messages as He did to the shepherds, but He sends messages to us all. We can learn about God and what He wants us to do from our parents and teachers.

PRAYER: Dear Lord, help us to be ready to listen to the messages you send us.

Shining Star Publications, Copyright © 1986, A division of Good Apple, Inc.

LEADER: Read Luke 2:9-16.

Sing together "Angels We Have Heard on High."

LEADER: The words of this song tell us what the angels sang on the night of Christ's birth. The Latin words *Gloria in excelsis Deo* mean Glory to God in the highest. They were first used as a hymn in 129 AD when Telespharus was the Bishop of Rome. He told people that they should solemnly sing the "Angels' Hymn" at their church services. The angels were sent by God to spread the Good News of Christ's birth.

PRAYER: Dear Lord, help us to be like the angels of old and share with others the Christmas message.

LEADER: Read Matthew 2:1-11.

Sing together "We Three Kings of Orient Are."

LEADER: "We Three Kings" is an American carol that was written to be acted out as a play. Lots of churches gave Epiphany plays, but John Hopkins thought his church's program would be special if the kings could tell their story in song. The king's journey was long and it was sometimes hard for them to follow the star. Sometimes it is hard for us to keep the light of Jesus in front of us.

PRAYER: Help us, Dear Lord, as we welcome Jesus into our hearts at Christmas, to resolve to try to follow Him through the year.

Shining Star Publications, Copyright © 1986, A division of Good Apple, Inc.

BRIGHT IDEAS FOR BIG SPACES

OVERSIZED ORNAMENTS

Cut ornaments from 12" x 18" construction paper. Cut two sheets of waxed paper slightly larger than the openings in the centers of the ornaments. Cut letters or snowflakes to go in the middle of the cutout areas. Iron them between the waxed paper and glue the waxed paper centers to the construction paper. "Tie" a piece of string to the top of each ornament shape. Fasten the ornaments to the wall. Tape the string to the ceiling so the ornament appears suspended.

TALL TREES

Cut 2 packages of green crepe paper into 4" strips. You will have two narrow strips left over. Twist them together and tape them to the wall for a trunk. Without unfolding the crepe paper, fringe both edges of each 4" strip. Open the crepe paper and fold the long strips in half. Fasten to the wall, stretching slightly so the fringe hangs down. Let your children decorate ornament shapes to hang on the "branches."

PAPER-PLATE PICTURES

Purchase enough paper plates so that you have one for each child. If you choose white plates, children can cut out and decorate green wreaths to fit within the plates. Green plates look attractive with photographs of the boys and girls glued to them. To make a tree, mount the plates to the wall as shown. Add a base. The plates can also be arranged in a wreath shape and decorated with a giant bow.

Shining Star Publications, Copyright © 1986, A division of Good Apple, Inc.

GIANT GINGERBODIES

Give each child in your room a part to play in the manger scene. (You can have an unlimited number of angels and shepherds.) Have the children draw around each other with a pencil on large pieces of brown wrapping paper. Also using pencil, add the appropriate details to make the gingerbodies recognizable as the characters they represent. Add a robe and head covering for Mary, crowns for the kings, etc. Thicken white paint with a little flour. Paint on "icing" details. Have one of the children make a gingerbaby Jesus. After the "icing" is dry, cut out the figures (be sure to leave a gingerbread edge showing) and arrange them on the wall in the hall.

As an alternative you can decide that "everybody is an angel" and decorate a whole hallway with gingerbody angels.

WINDOWS AND DOORS

Zephaniah prophesied that when the Messiah came the whole world would celebrate and that birds would "sing in the windows." We, too, can praise God from our windows, and like the shepherds "can make known abroad the sayings concerning the child." Spread the spirit of the season by decorating your windows using one or more of these ideas.

WINDOWS
  Speedy Stained Glass
  Pin-Prick Pictures
  Rainbows Bright 66

  Strip Stars
  Furnace Filter Flakes
  Bells in the Breeze 67

  Kaleidoscopes of Color
  Window Wreaths
  Wings in the Windows
  Other Pattern Possibilities 68

  Patterns. 69-74

DOORS
  To Be Wise Is. . .
  Good News
  Hand-y Wreaths 75

  The Best Gift
  The Heart of the Season
  Picture Perfect. 76

  The Very First Christmas 77

  Let Earth Receive Her King 78

Shining Star Publications, Copyright © 1986, A division of Good Apple, Inc.

WINDOWS

SPEEDY STAINED GLASS
(A project to occupy the hands of older students while you are presenting a lesson.)

Run off copies of the "God's Gift" and "Welcome Jesus" patterns on pages 69 and 70. Have the children carefully cut out the white areas. Back with red tissue paper. By alternating the direction in which you fasten the pictures, you can create a sort of patchwork effect that looks pretty on both sides.

PIN-PRICK PICTURES
(A nice soothing activity for small fingers.)

Copy the patterns on pages 71-74.
Cut out the center sections of the stencils. Use chalk to trace around them on dark-colored paper. Have the students place the colored paper on pieces of foam carpet padding. (Scraps are always available free from carpet salesmen.) Give each child a toothpick to use to poke dots along the chalk lines. Encourage children to complete the task so that when they are hung in the window, the picture is recognizable.

RAINBOWS BRIGHT
(Suitable for boys and girls of all ages.)

Run off copies of the patterns on pages 71-74, or let older children create their own simple patterns. Have the children tape the patterns to their desks. Give each child a piece of waxed paper to tape over the pattern. Provide 1" squares of colored tissue and glue brushes. Have each child apply a coat of white glue to the waxed paper in the shape of the pattern. Then have the children cover the picture with tissue, overlapping pieces and adding glue as necessary. Allow the pictures to dry overnight, and they'll pop right off the waxed paper. Details can be added with black marker. The tree is especially pretty if it is done in rainbow stripes, and similar rainbow stripes can be added to make rays descending from the star. Rows of color can be used to cover an entire window with a black silhouette of Joseph leading the donkey carrying Mary mounted in front of it. Some children may wish to make basic rainbows to remind the world that Jesus fulfills God's promise to be with us always.

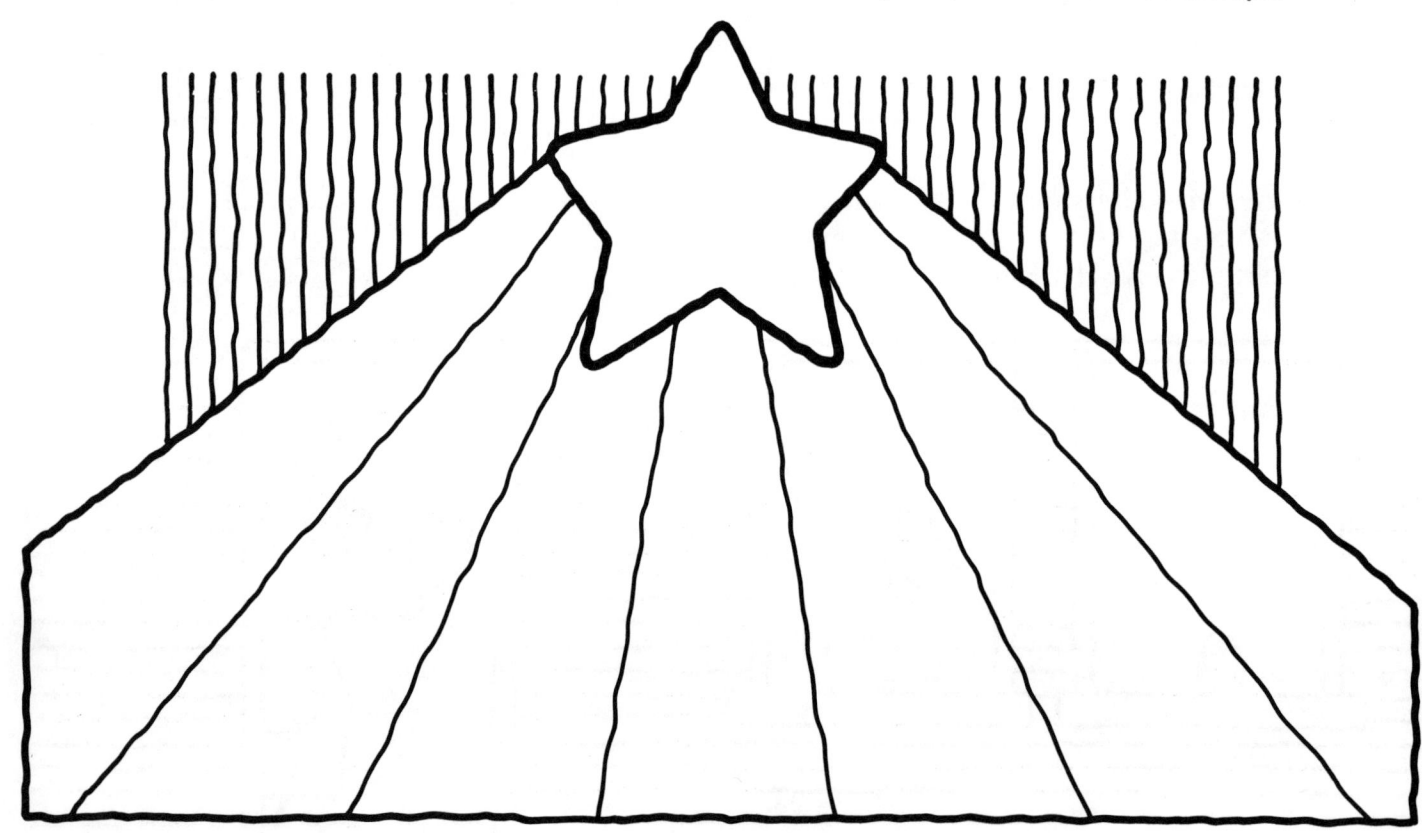

Shining Star Publications, Copyright © 1986, A division of Good Apple, Inc.

STRIP STARS

To make each star, you will need 5 one-half-inch strips of colored construction paper. Cut the strips 10" long for regular-sized windows. For multi-paned windows, cut strips smaller. Mark off a ½" section of each end of each strip for tabs. Fold the remainder of each strip into thirds (each 3"). Fold each strip into a triangle and glue down one tab to hold the triangle in place. When all the triangles are dry, arrange them as shown in the picture. Overlap the extra tabs ½" at all corners. Glue in place. Punch two holes, one opposite the other through the top of one triangle and thread a string through the holes to make a hanger for the ornament.

FURNACE FILTER FLAKES

A single furnace filter will make 12 window ornaments. Prior to class carefully remove the metal filter covers. Throw away the interior of the filters. Cut the metal into circular snowflake shapes. Cut two circles of waxed paper slightly smaller than each flake. Have the children cut out red and green circles to go inside the circles in the filter. After they glue the circles in the correct places on one sheet of waxed paper, place the second sheet on top of the first and iron the two sheets together. Staple the filter in place.

BELLS IN THE BREEZE

To make these ornaments, three children will have to work together. (This is not the time to ask your most particular child to work with someone who does not work carefully!) Enlarge the pattern so that it will fit on a 9" x 11" sheet of construction paper. Give each group of three children one red, one green, and one white sheet of paper. Have each group member cut out three bell shapes (one large, one medium-sized, and one small) from his piece of paper. Show them how to punch a hole to do the second and third cuttings. Have the children exchange bells within their groups so that they have three different-colored bells of increasing size. Give each child a piece of heavy sewing thread. Have him glue it to the center of the three bells. Tie a dime-store jingle bell to the bottom. Tape the string to the top of the window. If you have radiators in your room, the heat will make the bells move. The jingle bells will occasionally ring as they touch the windows.

Shining Star Publications, Copyright © 1986, A division of Good Apple, Inc.

KALEIDOSCOPES OF COLOR
(You may want to use this type of color dipping to make wrapping paper.)

Trace around a salad plate to make circles of white tissue paper (one for each student). Using a slightly smaller circle pattern, draw circles on black paper. Remove the center of the black circles to make frames.

Have each child fold his tissue in half and then in pie-shaped wedges. Have him fold over the wedge. (When working with younger children, you'll want to prefold the tissue for your students.) Set out TV-dinner trays (1 for every 4 children) into which you've poured food coloring. Have children dip corners of tissue into the food coloring. Allow the circles to dry (or iron open). Run a ribbon of glue around the inner edge of the black paper and glue the tissue in place.

WINDOW WREATHS
(These look good from both sides.)

Give each student a piece of bright green construction paper (9" x 12"). Show him how to fold the paper in half lengthwise to make a rectangle 4½" x 12". Mark a line one inch from the open side. Show the children how to cut 1" strips from the folded side to the line they've marked on the open edge. (Warn them not to cut past the line!) Next, have the children put glue on the inside of one 9" side and roll the other side over to meet the gluey surface. Pull the resulting tube into a ring and glue ends together, see illustration below. Red paper punch circles make good holly berries and a red bow adds a decorative touch.

WINGS IN THE WINDOWS
(Older children can produce beautiful metallic-looking decorations with this technique.)

Trace the angel pattern on page 64 (or use your own) onto shirt cardboard. Have children use pencil to draw on details and then color darkly with crayon leaving spaces between colors. Color both sides. Cover wing areas with foil. Brush with India ink. Wipe off with a damp cloth. Hang by strings into window.

OTHER PATTERN POSSIBILITIES
1. Spray snow inside stencils.
2. Use chalk to draw around stencils; paint with tempora.
3. Use stencils to make black paper frames. Sprinkle crayon shavings on waxed paper, cover with another sheet of waxed paper and then iron. Put inside black frame.
4. Use patterns to make shapes from colored paper. Decorate and hang by strings.

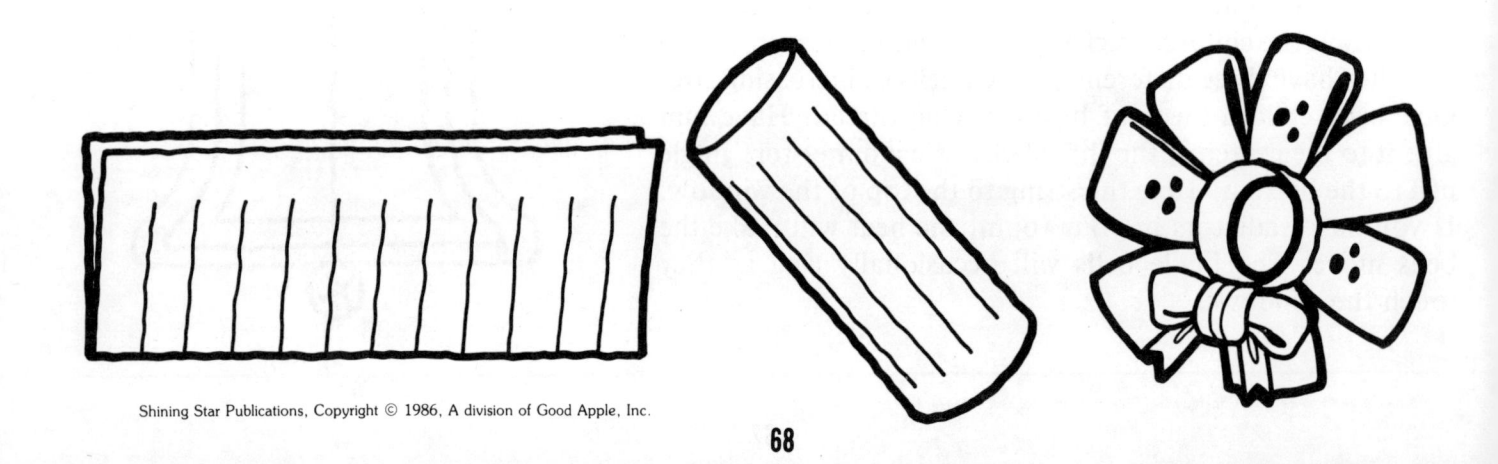

Shining Star Publications, Copyright © 1986, A division of Good Apple, Inc.

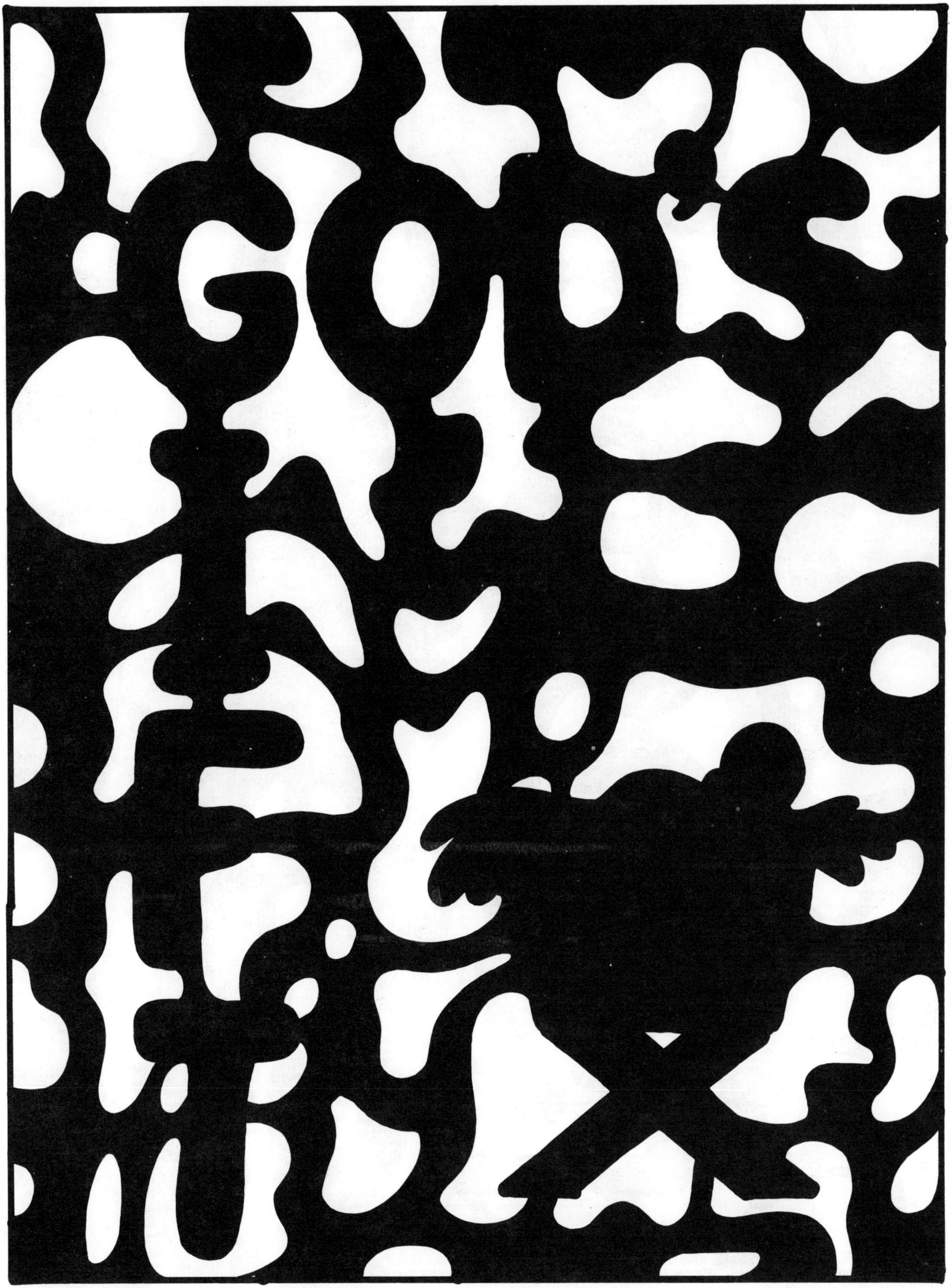

Shining Star Publications, Copyright © 1986, A division of Good Apple, Inc.

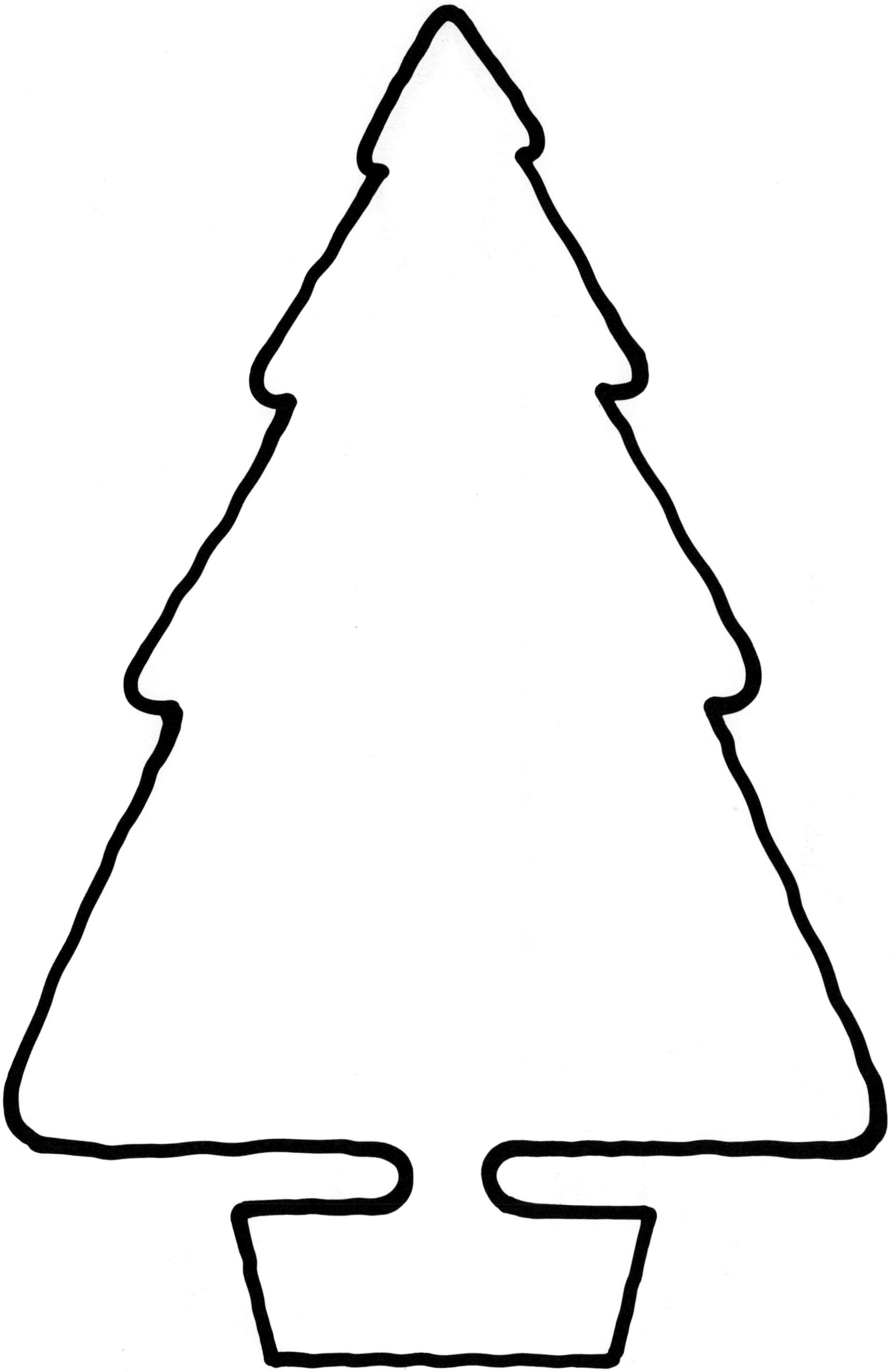

Shining Star Publications, Copyright © 1986, A division of Good Apple, Inc.
72

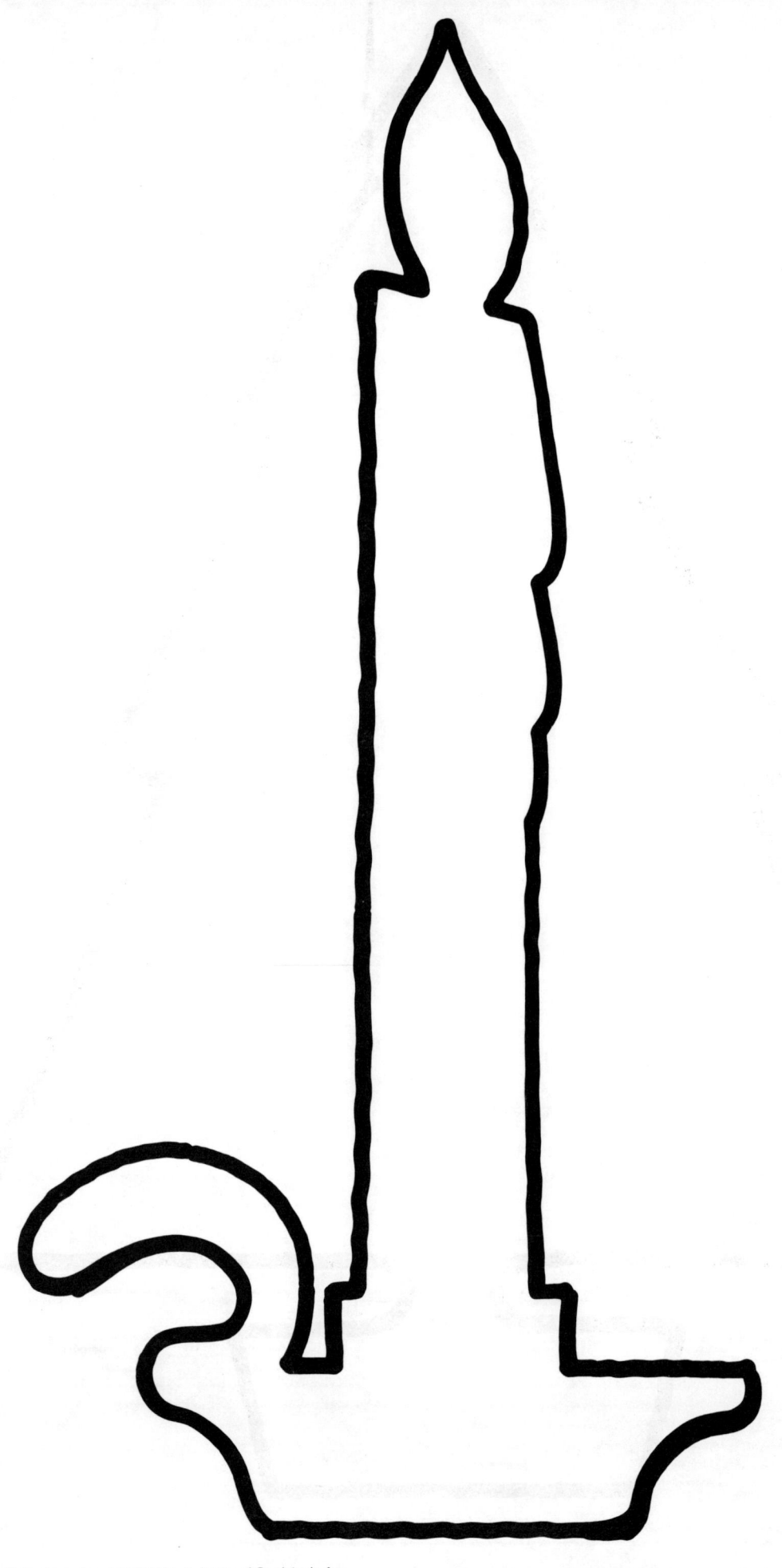

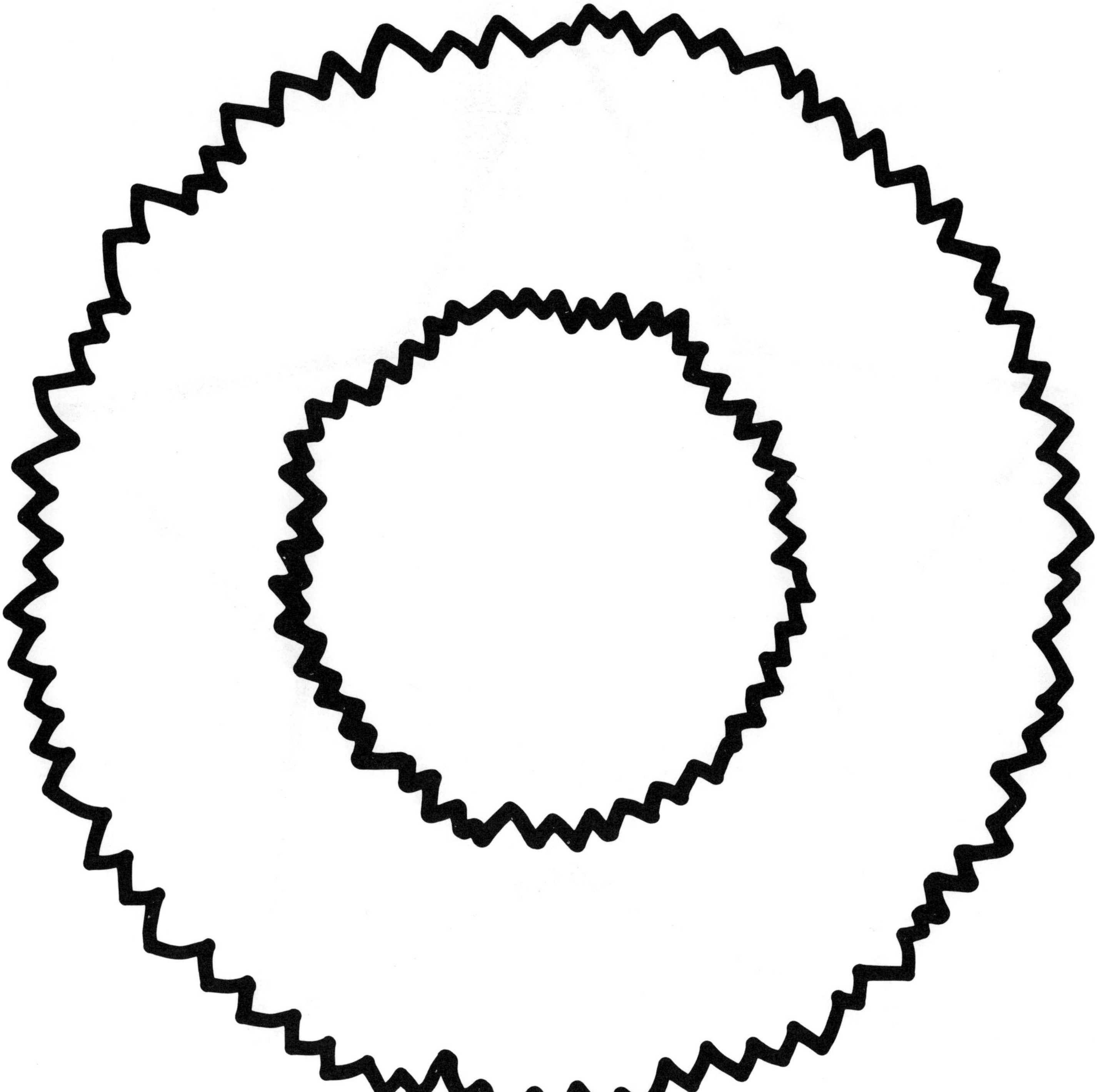

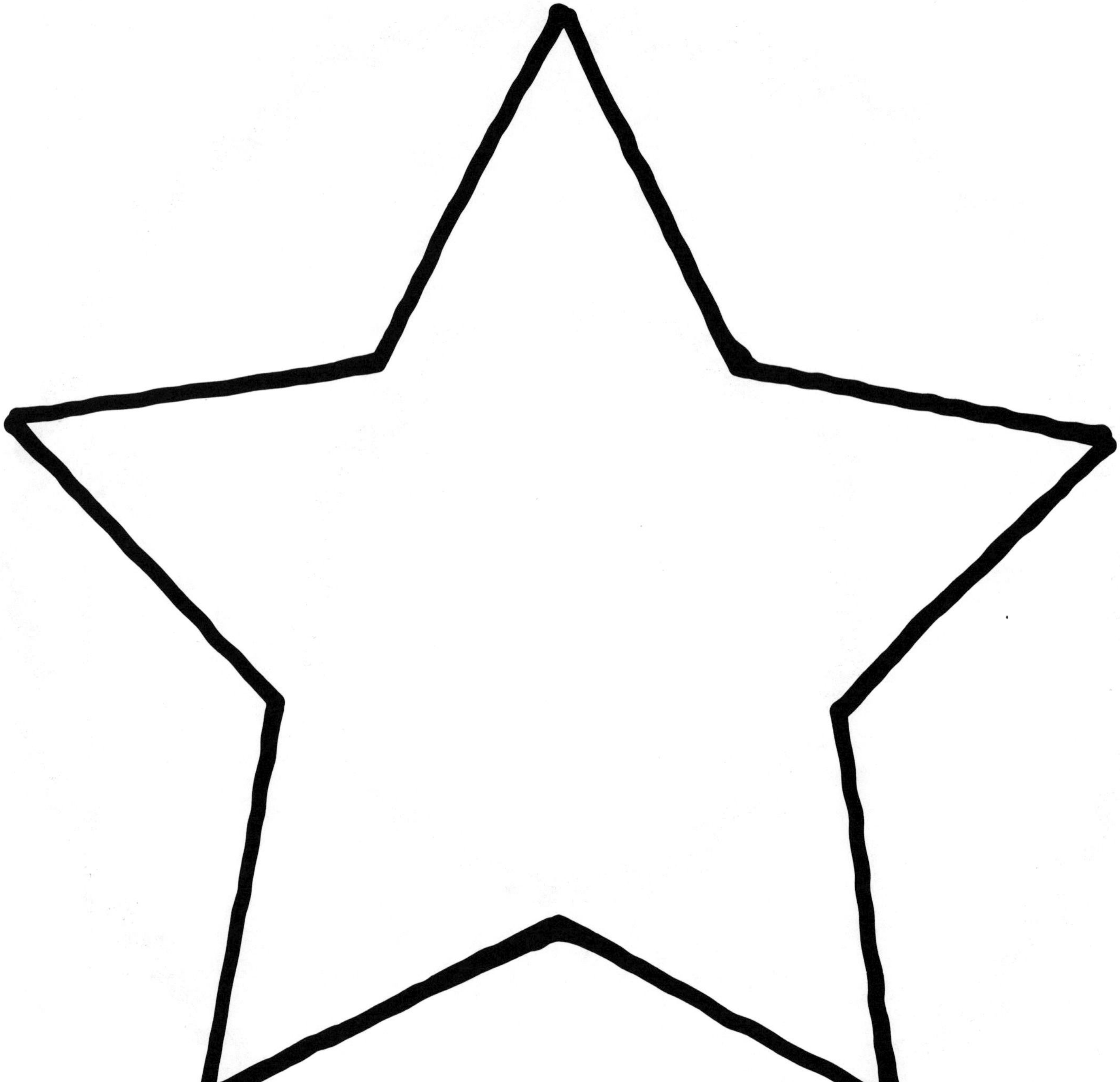

DOORS

TO BE WISE IS...
When you talk with the children about the visit of the wise men, ask them to define the word *WISE*. Write their definitions on irregular shapes of paper. (Older children can do their own writing.) Tape the responses on the door of your classroom with the title "To Be Wise Is . . ." You can modify this idea by entitling your door "Christmas Is . . ." You might also wish to combine the responses and send them home in booklet form for the parents to enjoy.

Cover your door with sheets of newspaper. The letters show up best on the classified sections. Cut letters from black paper. Talk with your students about the news they have been reading and hearing. Discuss how bad news results when people do not follow the teachings of the Lord.

HAND-Y WREATHS
Make this attractive wreath as a group project for kindergarteners. First trace around each child's hand on green paper. If children are able, have them cut out the hands. Glue the hands together, overlapping them to form a wreath shape. Add a bright red bow. The hand wreath can also be made by cutting a large piece of white paper for a background and letting children paint one hand green and then using the painted hand as a stamp to make a print for the wreath.

Shining Star Publications, Copyright © 1986, A division of Good Apple, Inc.

THE BEST GIFT

Select a small print wrapping paper and cover the entire door. Use crepe paper to make the ribbon and the bow. Before mounting the paper on the door, do the lettering with a wide black marker. You might select as an alternate verse I Timothy 4:14, "Neglect not the gift that is in thee . . . ." During class make coupons for the children to fill in promising gifts of themselves.

Cut a large tree from white paper and an identical tree from green paper. Cut out sections of the green to expose the white paper. Glue the green triangular shapes to the white paper. Use a large red marker to do the writing. Let each child cut out a heart to decorate the tree. Sing "Jesus Loves Me" or "Jesus Loves the Little Children" with your boys and girls.

PICTURE PERFECT

From a piece of roll paper, cut a large green Christmas tree. Make a yellow star for the top. Use an instant developing camera to take pictures of your students. Use a circle pattern to turn the pictures into Christmas balls. On the final day before vacation, use the photo balls on greeting cards that say "I wish you a Merry Christmas."

Shining Star Publications, Copyright © 1986, A division of Good Apple, Inc.

The very first Christmas the Lord God gave the Earth

1. A star to announce the Christ child's birth
2. Mary and Joseph
3. Wise Men
4. Kneeling Shepherds
5. Angel choirs
6. Doves a-cooing
7. Sheep a-baaing
8. Donkeys Braying
9. Cows a-mooing
10. Pigs an-oinking
11. Birds a-chirping
12. Ducks a-quacking

THE VERY FIRST CHRISTMAS

Cover the entire door with white paper. With a thick marker, write the heading on the top and then divide the remainder of the white area into twelve equal spaces. Assign each student to make one of the pictures you will need for the door decoration (one lamb, one pig, etc.). Glue the finished characters to the appropriate squares and do the rest of the writing. To ensure that the children make their animals the correct size, give them paper that is cut to the right size and ask them to use the entire piece of paper.

With older classes you might want to let the children decide what should go in each square.

(With a little adaptation, this can be sung to the tune of "The Twelve Days of Christmas.")

LET EARTH RECEIVE HER KING

Cover the door with gold wrapping paper or bright green roll paper. Enlarge the patterns of the churches around the world. Cut them from black paper. Use white chalk to add the details. Do the lettering with a wide black marker. Share with your class the Phillip Brooks poem "Everywhere, Everywhere Christmas Tonight." If you are teaching older children, you may wish to have groups give reports on Christmas celebrations around the world.

CEILINGS, FLOORS AND WELCOME MATS

"When they saw the star, they rejoiced with exceeding great joy."   Matthew 2:10

"And, lo, the angel of the Lord came upon them, and the glory of the Lord shone round about them . . . ." (Luke 2:9) The sky was filled with singing angels glorifying the birth of a baby born in a stable with hay upon the ground. Christmastime is for remembering all the events surrounding the most blessed moment in history. Celebrate Christmas with the decorations for ceilings and floors that follow and keep Jesus as the center of your Christmas fun.

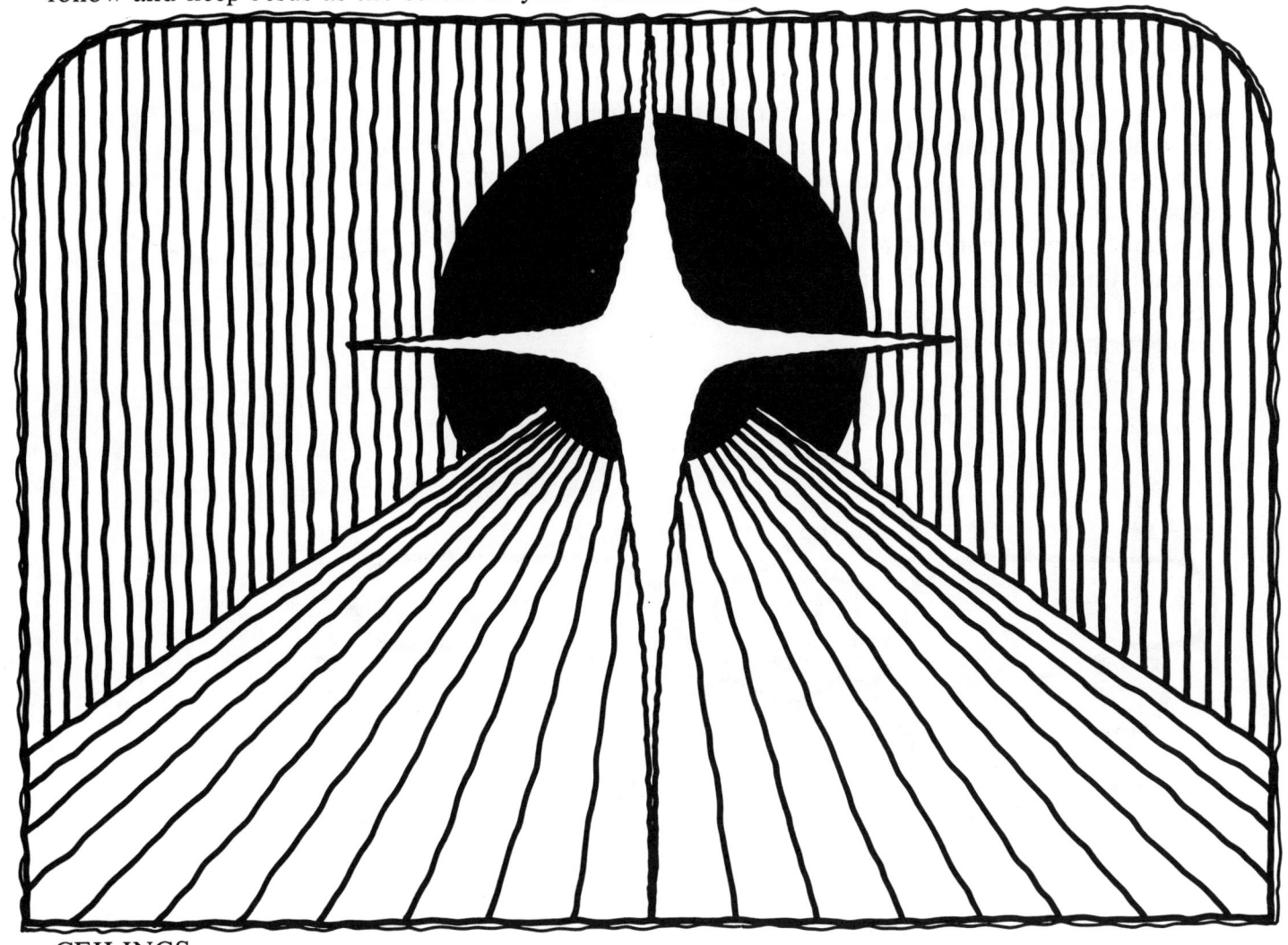

CEILINGS
- Angels Watching Over Me 80
- The Advent Wreath 81
- Donkey Piñata 82
- Manger Mobile 83
- Cut Paper Quickies 84

FLOORS
- Lights to Guide the Christ Child 85

WELCOME MATS
- Each Day Walk a Little Way 86

Shining Star Publications, Copyright © 1986, A division of Good Apple, Inc.

ANGELS WATCHING OVER ME

Trace angel patterns onto white oak tag. Make 7 of them for each student. Have the children cut out the angels, add yarn hair and decorate their angels. To join the angels in a ring, thread needle with double-strand black thread and knot. Place angels side by side so skirt tips overlap. Sew the skirt tips loosely together. Join wing tips using a 15" length of double thread knotted at the end for each pair of wings. Pass the needle through the wing tips and then between the double strand between tips. Pull the thread entirely through the loop. This will pull the wings together and give you a long double strand for hanging. Cut the star pattern from oaktag. Bring threads from the wings together. When the mobile hangs evenly, tie a knot in the strings. Push the knot through the center of the star and tie a knot above the star. Cut thread ends. Attach another double thread for hanging.

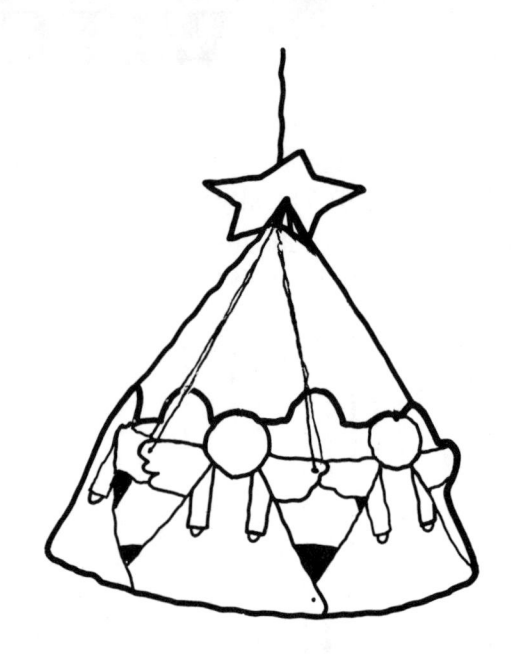

THE ADVENT WREATH

The Advent wreath is a cherished custom in many homes and churches. The circular shape of the wreath reminds us that God has no beginning and no end. The greens with which we decorate it represent eternal life and hope. Traditionally, the Advent wreath is lit on each of the four Sundays during Advent, but you can change the day you light it if your class does not meet on Sunday. Most Advent wreaths have three purple candles and one pink one. The purple signifies the time of preparation. The pink candle, which is customarily lit on the final Sunday before Christmas, represents the joy we feel because God loved us so much that He sent Jesus into the world.

Because you will probably want to use your Advent wreath year after year, it is worth the time and expense to make a good sturdy one. Begin with a wreath shape that has been cut out of ½" plywood. The size will depend upon where you want to hang the wreath. If you do not have the tools needed to cut the wreath, most lumberyards will cut the plywood for a minimal charge. Cut pieces of medium-gauge wire three times the diameter of the wreath. Drill four evenly spaced holes about ½" from the outer edge of the wreath. Thread one wire through two opposite holes and the second wire through the other two holes. Bring the wires together above the wreath and twist. Make a hook for hanging from the twisted top. Nail four metal bottle tops to the wreath to serve as candle holders. Cover the wreath with chicken wire.

When you are ready to set up the wreath for the Advent season, drip a little wax into each candle holder. Hold the candles in place until the wax hardens. Finally, fill in the holes in the chicken wire with fresh evergreens. Try not to let any of the wood show.

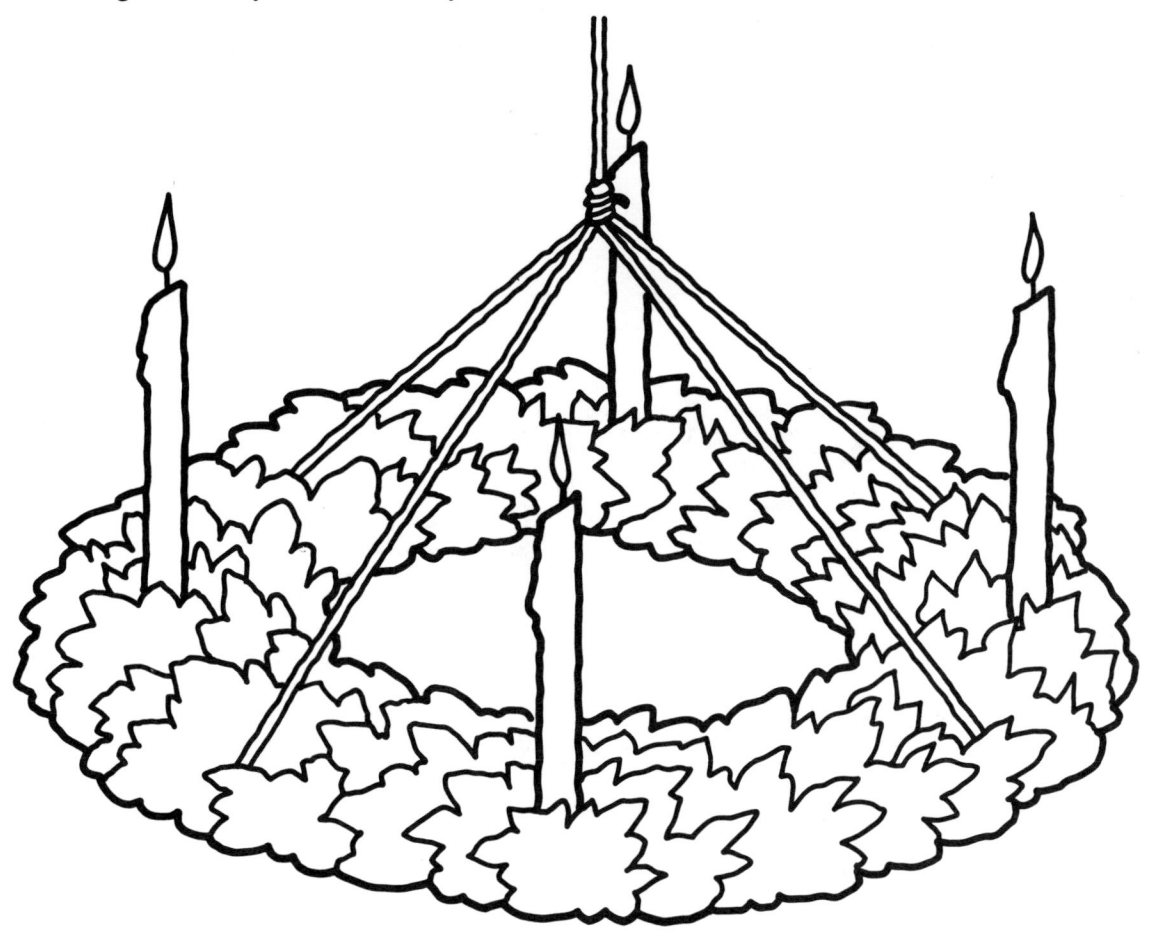

A simple Advent wreath for your students to make is described on page 6.

DONKEY PIÑATA

The piñata chosen for the posada is often in the shape of a donkey. Let each child make a donkey decoration for the hall and then allow your students to break your filled sample on the final day before vacation.

Begin by giving each child a balloon. Have the children blow up and tie the balloons and then put them in brown lunch sacks. Tie the ends of the sacks. Then show the children how to make heads and legs from toilet paper tubes. Use a tube for each leg and make the head by cutting, folding and taping tube as shown. Stick the ends of the sack into the head/neck tube. Tape together. Cover donkey with two layers of glue-soaked paper towel. Allow to dry.

The following week carefully cut a hole in the back of the donkey. (If the children are not going to fill their piñatas, you do not need to have them do this step.) Lift off the lid. Paint the donkey and the lid. Glue on ears and tail. If you have time (and money), decorate each donkey with strips of tissue or crepe paper. Fill your sample piñata with treats. Top with the lid. Tie a rope around the neck of the piñata so you can hang or hold it high. Let blindfolded children try breaking the piñata with a rolled-up newspaper. To ensure that everyone has a turn, move piñata up and away as children swing at it on their first turns.

MANGER MOBILE

For each mobile cut a strip of oak tag 2" wide and 36" long. Bend the oak tag to form a circle and staple it in place. Punch four evenly spaced holes in the frame. Cut two pieces of string 36" long. Thread the first piece through two holes on opposite sides of the ring. Thread the other piece through the other holes. Bring the ends of the strings together above the mobile frame and tie them together. Bend a paper clip and hook it through the top strings for a hanger. Punch four more holes between the first holes. Duplicate the little people below so that each child has a set of four. Have the children color their little people pictures and then tie strings to them. Help them tie the strings through the holes in the frames.

Shining Star Publications, Copyright © 1986, A division of Good Apple, Inc.

CUT PAPER QUICKIES

All these decorations can be made in a few minutes at the end of a class period. They look pretty as they sway from the ceiling.

TREE SHAPE
(Paper-punch circles can be glued to the "branches" for decorations or sticky-back stars can be added.)
Fold a square of green construction paper in half diagonally and then in half again. Cut on the broken lines as shown. Open out carefully. Hang from the small square in the center. Pull the "branches" down gently to form the tree shape.

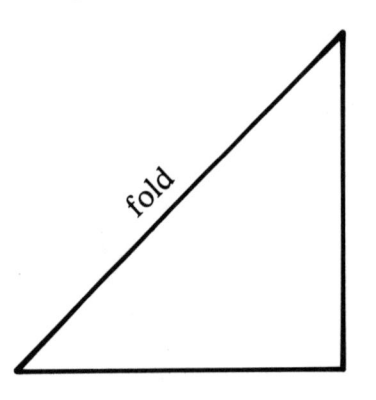

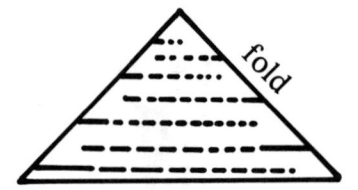

BIG BALLS
Begin with a 9" circle. Fold as shown and cut on the broken lines. Unfold carefully. Fasten from the small piece at the top. Pull the sides down and glue or staple the bottom together.

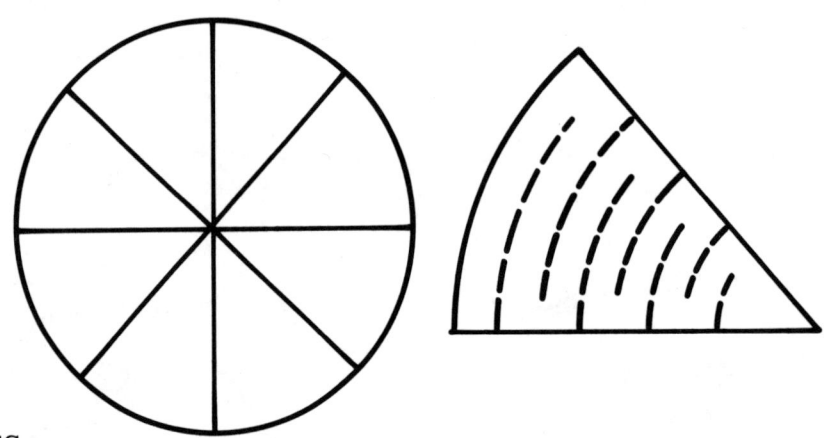

SWINGING CIRCLES
Begin with a 9" circle. Fold and cut as shown. When you open the circle, fold alternating circles to the front and to the back.

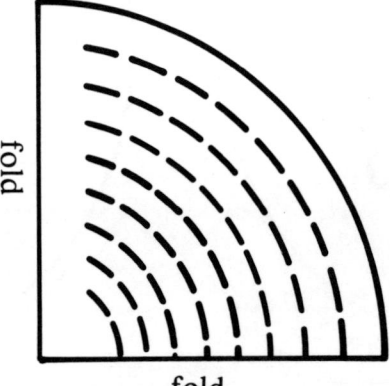

Shining Star Publications, Copyright © 1986, A division of Good Apple, Inc.

LIGHTS TO GUIDE THE CHRIST CHILD

Placing a light in the window at Christmastime is a custom in many parts of the world. Candles are used as a part of our Christmas decorations to light the Christ Child's way. Candles play an important role in celebrations in the churches. Candlelight services are held on Christmas Eve in thousands of churches throughout the United States. In some communities, families carry the candles home to light again so that Christ will know that He is welcome in their homes.

GIANT CANDLES

Candle makers made the candles used at Christmastime especially tall and thick. They did not want them to burn down on Christmas Eve before the festivities of the night came to an end. You can make some candles that will never burn out even if you put them on the floor of your Sunday School hall. Begin by looking in the phone book for the heating and air conditioning dealers who live in your town. You may even know of one who attends your church. Ask if you can borrow some heating pipes for the holiday season. Assure them that you will not damage them and promise to return them immediately after Christmas. The chimney pipes generally come in 4' and 8' lengths. The smaller ones are easier to transport but large enough to be impressive. Cover each pipe with roll paper. Make a flame by wadding newspaper into a flame shape, taping it with masking tape and then covering it with 2 or 3 layers of paper towel that has been dipped in glue. When the glue is dry, paint the flame and set it in the candle base.

LUMINARIES

In Mexico and the Southwest, people light the way for Jesus with luminaries. To make luminaries for your church, you will need a supply of sand. Although construction sand is cheaper, if you live in a cold climate it may be frozen and you may have to purchase sand from a lumberyard. Fill brown lunch sacks about ⅓ of the way up with damp sand. Roll back the tops of the bags to make cuffs. Push candles into the damp sand. The sand will keep the candles from tipping and the sacks will not catch on fire. Light luminaries along your hall on the evening of your Christmas program. Save them to set outside the church for the Christmas Eve candlelight service.

WELCOME MATS

Have children submit design ideas for welcome mats that can be placed outside their rooms. Select a design to enlarge on a 12" x 18" sheet of white poster board. Use paint or marker to color in the welcome mat. Secure it to the floor with rings of masking tape. Carefully cover the entire welcome mat with clear Con-Tact paper. Allow the Con-Tact paper to extend about 2" on all sides. This will secure it well enough to withstand the traffic it will be subject to.

EACH DAY WALK A LITTLE WAY TOWARD BETHLEHEM

For each day from the first day of Advent to either Christmas Eve or Christmas Day, cut a set of footprints. Fasten the footprints to the floor with rings of masking tape. Carefully cover the footprints with clear Con-Tact paper so they will stay fresh until the final day. Make a dummy of a child. If you have an extra banner holder, you can use that as a base. The bottom from the volleyball stand in a gym works well, too. Dress the dummy in child's clothes. Paint facial features and add yarn hair. Place your dummy on the first set of footprints. As Advent progresses, move him closer to Bethlehem. Bethlehem could be a mural of a manger (see page 59) or the creche that your church displays at Christmastime.

ORNAMENTS FOR ALL AGES

    A Tree for All Ages 88

PRESCHOOL PROJECTS
    Little Drums for Little Drummers
    Sweet Silver Bells
    Nature's Own Ornaments
    Tiny Tot Tinsel 89

PRIMARILY FOR PRIMARY
    Rigatoni Wreaths
    Cookie Sheet Christmas Ornaments
    Christmas Churches
    Baked Babies 90
    Christ the King Crowns 91

INTERMEDIATE IDEAS
    Recycled Christian Ornaments
    Christmas Cookies 91
    The Smells of Christmas
    Candy Canes
    Mother and Child 92
    Birds and Butterflies 93
    Picture Frame Ornaments 94

HARD ENOUGH FOR JUNIOR HIGH
    Pom-pom Camels 94
    Tin Can Lanterns
    Wonderful Words of Life
    Macrame Angels 95
    Two for One Ornament 96

Shining Star Publications, Copyright © 1986, A division of Good Apple, Inc.

A TREE FOR ALL AGES

Long before the birth of Jesus, both the Tree of Life and the Tree of Knowledge of Good and Evil are mentioned in the second book of Genesis. The Jesse Tree (see page 11) helps us picture the genealogy of the people who waited for the birth of a Saviour.

No one knows for sure who invented the first Christmas tree, but decorated trees and branches have been used at Christmastime for many centuries. Many legends credit Martin Luther with having the first Christmas tree. People say that he decorated his tree with candles as a reminder of the stars above Bethlehem, apples as a reminder of Adam and Eve and flat wafers as a reminder that Jesus came to be the "bread of life." Trees decorated with these symbols were called Christbaum.

In Germany where Martin Luther lived, there were lots of fir trees, so perhaps the first Christmas tree looked like the traditional American evergreen trees. Now Christmas is celebrated with many different types of trees throughout the world. In Africa, Christian families sometimes cut oil palms and decorate them with red bells. In Japan, bonsai trees are sometimes decorated with bright paper ornaments.

The Swedish probably made the first artificial trees when they notched pieces of wood and placed wooden ornaments on the resulting branches. The wooden trees kept the triangular shape that is used to represent the Trinity. If you do not want to purchase a real tree, you will certainly want to set up an artificial one. On the following pages are some suggestions for decorations your students can make for your church tree or to take home to decorate their family trees.

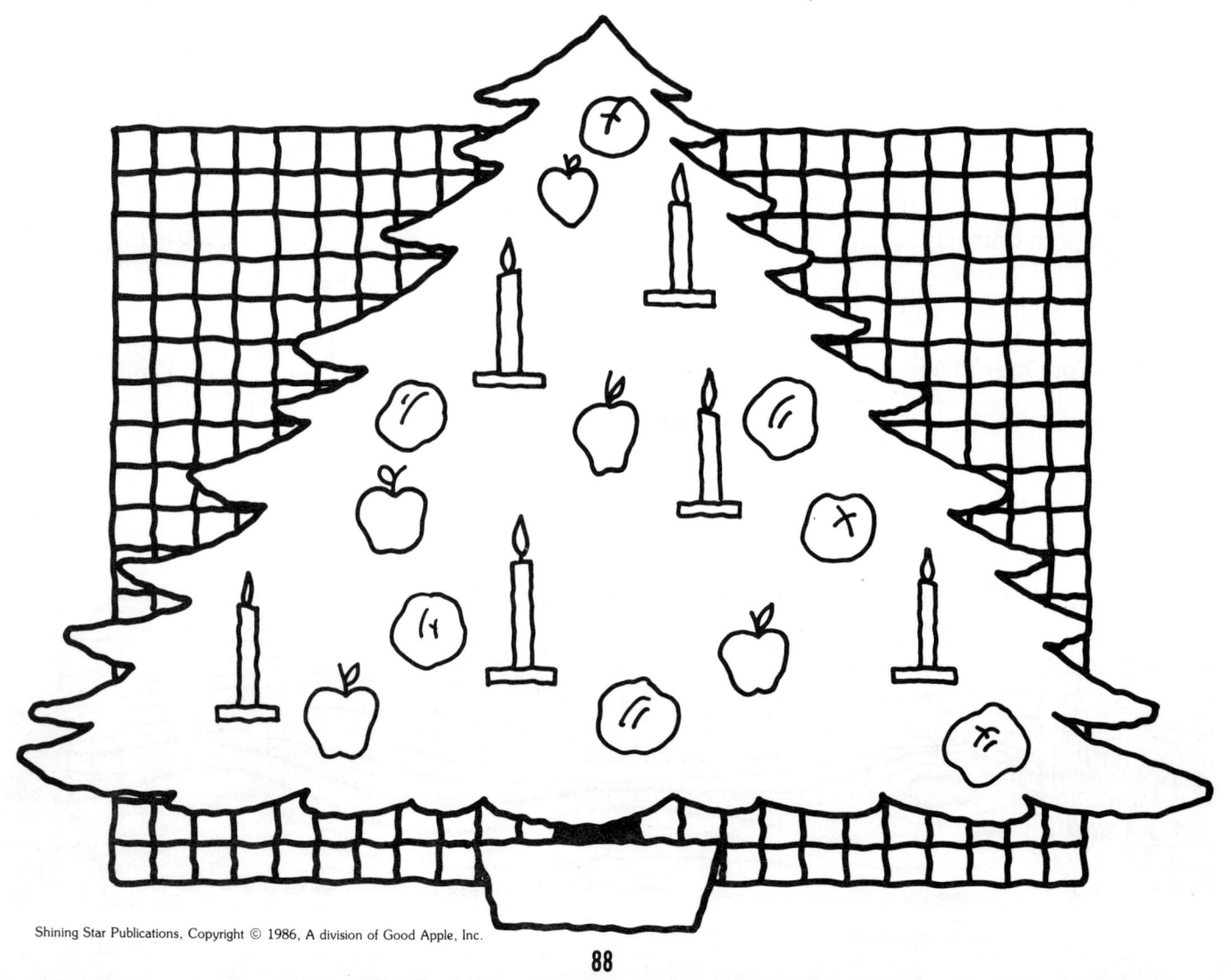

Shining Star Publications, Copyright © 1986, A division of Good Apple, Inc.

PRESCHOOL PROJECTS

LITTLE DRUMS FOR LITTLE DRUMMERS
Prior to class, collect a supply of styrofoam spools, the kind that come with sewing thread on them. (You might ask the home economics teacher at your local high school to save some for you.) Also, precut strips of colored paper to go around the drums and circles of white paper for the tops. Share Ezra Jack Keats' book *The Little Drummer Boy* with your children, and have them glue the paper on the drums. Give each child two matches to glue onto the top of each drum for drumsticks. A regular metal tree ornament hook will stick into the styrofoam so the drum can be hung on the tree.

SWEET SILVER BELLS
For each bell you will need a composition flowerpot. (The florist with whom the church does business might donate them.) An alternative is to cut the cups from composition muffin tins that come inside the new muffin mixes. You will also need squares of foil large enough to cover the insides and outsides of the pots and small jingle bells that have been tied to 6" strings. Show the children how to cover the pots with the foil. Poke a hole in the top of each covered pot and insert the jingle bell. Bring the extra string down to make a loop and tie a knot.

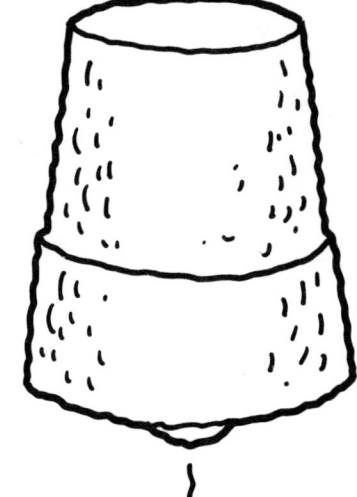

NATURE'S OWN ORNAMENTS
Greek children paint walnuts to decorate the ships they carry from house to house on St. Nicholas Day. Let your preschoolers paint walnuts with gold paint. (It's easiest to tie the string around the nut, in the crack between halves, before the children do their painting.) As an alternative have the children paint pinecones as pioneer children used to do. While the paint is still wet, sprinkle glitter onto the cone.

TINY TOT TINSEL
Share with the children the legend of the spiders who wanted to see the pretty Christmas tree. They crept all over the tree leaving cobwebs. When the Christ Child came to bless the tree, He knew that the family would not be happy to find cobwebs in the tree so He touched the webs and they turned into silver.

Have the children cut silver spiderwebs from the inside of cereal boxes. Cutting straight lines is good practice for eye-hand coordination for small children, and the tinsel looks pretty on the church Christmas tree.

Shining Star Publications, Copyright © 1986, A division of Good Apple, Inc.

PRIMARILY FOR PRIMARY

RIGATONI WREATHS
Die rigatoni in food coloring mixed with a little alcohol. (Shake in a large peanut butter jar and spread on a cookie sheet to dry.) Have children string the rigatoni using about five to a wreath. Using curling ribbon, help them make bows for the tops of the wreaths. Remind the boys and girls that the wreath is a symbol that God is eternal.

COOKIE SHEET CHRISTMAS ORNAMENTS
Begin by cutting a piece of cardboard (2½" by 3") for each child. Have each child cover the cardboard with foil as if he were wrapping a present. He will not need glue or tape. Give each child a sheet on which you have run off four angels. Have him cut out the angels and color them brown. He can use black pen to draw faces on his angels. Fasten the "gingerbread angels" to the foil "cookie sheet." Punch a hole for hanging and add a red ribbon. (See pattern on page 93.)

CHRISTMAS CHURCHES
Begin by copying this pattern (page 96) onto a piece of light cardboard. Trace around it on oak tag, making enough churches so all of your students have one. Have the children color the churches and glue them to the flat side of clip clothespins. The opening of the clothespin should be at the bottom of the church so that it can be clipped on a branch of the Christmas tree. When you send the ornaments home, you might want to send a copy of the church's Christmas schedule in each clip.

(You can make more elaborate churches by adding tiny toothpick crosses or a little cotton for snow.)

BAKED BABIES
These darling ornaments are made from two cotton balls dipped in a mixture of flour and water (about pancake batter consistency) that has been colored with a bit of red food coloring. On a greased cookie sheet, arrange the cotton balls, elongating one for the body. Bake in a 350 degree oven for about 10 minutes (until the babies seem hard to the touch). Let cool. Have children use pen to draw on the features. Have them wrap the babies in a small piece of flannel. Glue will hold the flannel in place. Make a slip knot and tie it around the baby's neck to make a hanger to hang from the tree.

Shining Star Publications, Copyright © 1986, A division of Good Apple, Inc.

CHRIST THE KING CROWNS
Before class, cut enough strips of cardboard tube so that each child has a piece 3" high. (The wide tubes that come inside wrapping paper are the ideal size.) Have the children cut the points on their crowns. It helps if they draw first so the points are evenly spaced. Have them glue on yarn decorations. When glue is dry, have them cover the entire crown with half a sheet of paper towel which has been dipped in slightly diluted glue. They will need to mold the gluey paper with their fingers so the decorations show. Allow the crowns to dry before you have the children paint them. Be sure that the paint is not too watery or the crowns will become mushy.

INTERMEDIATE IDEAS

RECYCLED CHRISTIAN ORNAMENTS
To make these ornaments, you will need a supply of old ribbon-covered styrofoam balls. If you don't have old ones, you can buy them inexpensively. You will also need one package of Christian wrapping paper, the type sold at Bible book stores. Prior to class, collect an electric frying pan, some paraffin and an old metal tennis ball can. Have your students cut small pictures from the wrapping paper and glue them to the balls. While you are melting the paraffin in the tennis ball can, have the children tie strings to the loops at the tops of the balls. Let each child carefully dip his ball into the melted paraffin. Withdraw it and let it cool. When the paraffin is hard, untie the strings and hang on the tree with metal Christmas tree hooks.

Old styrofoam ornaments can also be recycled with yarn. Wind glue-covered balls with lengths of bright-colored yarn. With practice, the patterns the children make can become quite complex.

CHRISTMAS COOKIES
According to many legends, Martin Luther decorated the first Christmas tree with apples and the wafers (hosts) that were used at communion. Through the years the wafers changed to cookies and were made in the shapes of many other Christmas symbols. Follow this recipe to make edible ornaments.

Cream together:
  1 c. sugar
  ¾ c. margarine

Then add:
  2 eggs   2½ c. flour
  1 tsp. vanilla   1 tsp. baking powder

Refrigerate at least one hour. Roll dough on lightly floured cloth. Cut with cookie cutters. Place on cookie sheets. Paint with egg yolk paint (1 egg yolk and ¼ tsp. water—divide mixture and tint with food coloring). Bake at 400 degrees about 8 minutes. (Makes about 3 dozen cookies.)

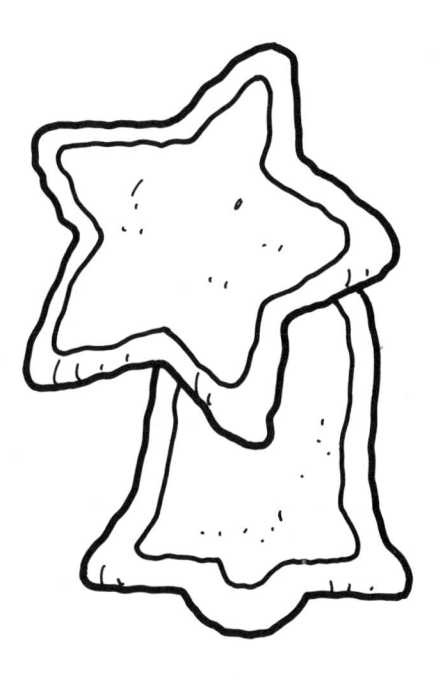

THE SMELLS OF CHRISTMAS

The very first Christmas trees were decorated with apples and circular wafers representing hosts. Apples were also used to decorate the trees of the settlers of the American West. The pomander balls that they made served as a reminder of the fragrances and spices that were considered so valuable at the time of Christ's birth. For each ball you will need a small apple and about 1½ cups of cloves. You will also need one large box of powdered cinnamon. (Try to buy the cloves from a store that sells bulk spices.) To save class time, tie thread loops to the stems of the apples before the children come. (If there are no stems, use a needle to "sew" through the cores.) Have the children push their cloves into the apples. When they have completely covered the apples, shake them one at a time in a lunch sack filled with powdered cinnamon. Hang ornaments from low branches.

CANDY CANES

The candy canes that decorate our Christmas trees are reminders of the crooks used by the shepherds who first saw the star. Your children can make these paper canes in only a few minutes. Begin with a 6" square of paper. Have children use red crayon or marker to draw the lines as shown in the picture. (If they fold the square in half diagonally, it will be easier to keep their lines straight.) Roll up the paper beginning at corner B. Bend the top to look like a cane and fasten the ends with glue.

MOTHER AND CHILD

To make Mary, each child will need a clothespin (not the pinch type). Each child will also need a peanut for Baby Jesus. With a ruler, measure the height of the clothespin. Cut a square of fabric the same measurement. With a needle and thread, run a gathering stitch along the top of the square. Glue the center back seam together. Gather the fabric and tie it around the clothespin. Use acrylic paint or markers to make a face. Glue on some yarn for hair. Glue a piece of ribbon around the neck. Cut arms from felt. Sew them to the sides of Mary's robe. Cut a second square of material (blue is the traditional color) the same size as the first square. Glue it to the top of Mary's head and in a few places where it covers the robe. Make Baby Jesus by painting the peanut, drawing a face and wrapping it in a soft piece of flannel. Glue Mary's hands to the peanut.

Shining Star Publications, Copyright © 1986, A division of Good Apple, Inc.

BIRDS AND BUTTERFLIES

Both symbols of God, birds and butterflies make bright additions to the Christmas tree. Begin by making craft dough: combine 2 cups flour, 1 cup salt and 1 cup water. Knead dough 2 or 3 minutes. (If you are making the dough in advance, be sure to keep it well-covered.) Give each child a square of foil and a full soup can to use as a rolling pin. Have the children roll the dough to a ¼" thickness. Using a sharp knife point (not a serrated knife), cut out the patterns. For the butterfly unfold a pipe cleaner and refold to make the antennae. Dip into water and insert into the butterfly between the wings. Moisten the back of the body and fasten it in place with the head covering the inserted antennae. Insert a paper clip into one of the wings for hanging. For the bird, insert a paper clip along the back between the head and tail. Moisten the back of the wing and press into place. Allow two days for the ornaments to dry or dry them overnight in a 200° degree oven. Paint birds and butterflies with red and green acrylic paint. Encourage children to be creative in their use of colors.

Angel Pattern
Cookie Sheet Ornament
page 90

Shining Star Publications, Copyright © 1986, A division of Good Apple, Inc.

PICTURE FRAME ORNAMENTS

Parents love to receive picture ornaments because each time they are put on the tree they bring back memories of past Christmases. Prior to class take pictures of your students or ask parents to provide them. Have each child unwrap six peppermint candies and arrange them on a cookie sheet to form a wreath. Bake in a 250 degree oven until the candies melt together. (Time depends upon the candies you use.) Allow the wreaths to cool slightly and then carefully remove them from the pans. With curly ribbon make a bow and glue the picture behind the opening. (You can glue a piece of felt to the back if you wish.)

As an alternative, make heart-shaped frames using the craft dough recipe on page 93 to which you have added red food coloring. Cut the pictures with a circle pattern smaller than the heart. Press the circle pattern into the heart dough and with your finger push down the dough in that area. When the dough is dry, glue the picture into the indentation. Write the child's name and the date on the ornament with white paint.

HARD ENOUGH FOR JUNIOR HIGH

POM-POM CAMELS

For each camel you will need three ¼", five ½", fourteen 1", four 1½" and five 2" gold pom-poms. You will also need gold felt, tiny black beads and 18-gauge wire. String the pom-poms on the legs as shown. Fill in the spaces by gluing strips of felt around the wire. String the pom-poms for the neck, head and back as shown. Glue the two sections together. Cut out ears and eyelids. Glue them in place. Glue on the eyes. Attach clear fishing line for the hanger.

Shining Star Publications, Copyright © 1986, A division of Good Apple, Inc.

TIN CAN LANTERNS

Prior to meeting with your students, fill metal juice cans with water and freeze them. Ask each child to bring a hammer and a cookie sheet from home. Provide a nail for each student and stimulate their creativity with some pictures of Mexican tin lanterns. Have the children place their cans on the trays and nail through the metal into the ice. (The ice keeps the can from bending while the boys and girls are nailing.) After the decorations have been completed, have the children nail two holes through which they can insert a piece of wire for a handle. In addition to being used as tree ornaments, these little lanterns can be used as candle holders by putting candle stubs inside the cans.

WONDERFUL WORDS OF LIFE

To make these ornaments, you only need waxed paper, white glue and either acrylic paint or paint markers. Have your students choose a Christmas word and write it in cursive on a piece of scrap paper (approximately 1½" by 5"). Put the waxed paper over the word and trace over it with white glue. Allow it to dry several days before painting it. As an alternative you can have the children put glue into jar lids (the kind without grooves) and when it dries paint the letters of the word on it.

You might want to share with your boys and girls some of the meanings that have been given to the word *Noel*. It is related to the French word *natalis* meaning *birth*. The English word *Nowell* means all is well.

MACRAME ANGELS

For each angel your students will need a 1" macrame bead and two pieces of white yarn, one 12" long and one 24" long. First, have your students draw faces on the beads with acrylic paint or fine-tipped markers. (They look especially cute if the cheeks are painted pink.) While faces are drying, have your students fold both pieces of yarn in half. Next, show them how to make a simple knot (right over left) about two inches from the loop at the top of the longest piece. Two inches below that make a second single knot. Allow the yarn between the loops to extend about 1" on either side. Place the short piece of yarn on top of and in the center of the longer piece. Use a single knot to tie the right piece of the long yarn loop to the right piece of the short yarn loop. Then tie the left two pieces together in the same way. Slip the top loops through the hole in the bead. Use the loop from the shorter piece of yarn for hanging the ornament.

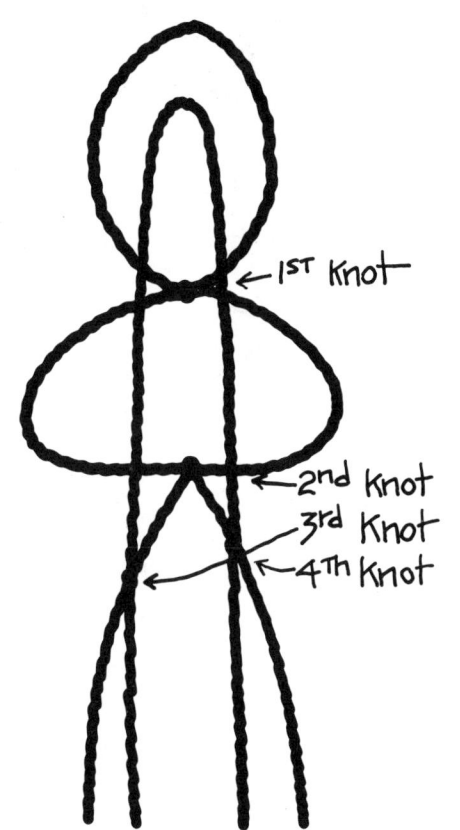

Shining Star Publications, Copyright © 1986, A division of Good Apple, Inc.

TWO FOR ONE ORNAMENT

Combine the star and the wreath symbols to make a single ornament. Each student will need a plastic margarine lid, and you will need plain green Christmas wrapping paper (or origami paper) and tiny print or dotted tissue paper. For the stuffing you will need polyester stuffing or cotton. Begin by having each child cut out 5 triangles from the green paper and a circle 1" larger than the margarine tub lid from the print paper. Next, have each child find the exact center of the circular paper. Give him a pentagon pattern to trace around, being sure that he has matched the center of the pattern and the center of the wreath. Have him glue the five triangles in place. While the glue is drying, use the pentagon to draw and cut out a pentagon from the center of the plastic lid. Place a little cotton near the edge of the outside of the plastic lid. Cover the lid with the print paper, centering carefully. Glue the excess paper to the back of the lid. Make some slits in the center so that you can pull the excess paper through there also. Cut a piece of green paper to cover the back. Glue it in place.

Church Ornament Pattern
page 90

Shining Star Publications, Copyright © 1986, A division of Good Apple, Inc.